The Methuen Drama Book of Suffrage Plays

Naomi Paxton is an actress, writer and researcher. She trained at Goldsmiths College, University of London and at the Royal Scottish Academy of Music and Drama and has performed professionally in the West End, on tour in the UK and internationally. She produced 'Knickerbocker Glories', a season of three one-act suffrage comedies, in London in 2010 and is currently a PhD student in the Drama Department of the University of Manchester.

The Methuen Drama Book of Suffrage Plays

How the Vote Was Won

Lady Geraldine's Speech

Pot and Kettle

Miss Appleyard's Awakening

Her Vote

The Mother's Meeting

An Anti-Suffragist or The Other Side

Tradition

Edited and with an introduction by
NAOMI PAXTON

B L O O M S B U R Y
LONDON · NEW DELHI · NEW YORK · SYDNEY

Bloomsbury Methuen Drama

An imprint of Bloomsbury Publishing Plc

50 Bedford Square	1385 Broadway
London	New York
WC1B 3DP	NY 10018
UK	USA

www.bloomsbury.com

Bloomsbury is a registered trade mark of Bloomsbury Publishing Plc

This collection first published in Great Britain in 2013 by
Bloomsbury Methuen Drama
Reprinted 2014

How the Vote Was Won © Lady Bower 1908
Pot and Kettle © Lady Bower 1909
Introduction © Methuen Drama 2013

The editor would like to thank her family, colleagues and partner for
their continued encouragement and support.

British Library Cataloguing-in-Publication Data
A catalogue record for this book is available from the British Library.

ISBN: PB:	978-1-4081-7658-0
EPDF:	978-1-4081-7660-3
EPUB:	978-1-4081-7659-7

Library of Congress Cataloging-in-Publication Data
A catalog record for this book is available from the Library of Congress.

Printed and bound in Great Britain

Contents

List of Illustrations

Introduction

There were over 400 female playwrights in Britain between the years 1900 and 1920, a period which witnessed enormous political and social change.[1] Challenged and invigorated by emerging 'New Woman' theatre and literature, many women writers were also inspired by their political beliefs. Often frustrated by the opportunities, both on and off stage, that were available to them in the predominantly male run professional theatre business, they chose to use the theatre to represent and debate the contemporary issues that concerned them.

The plays featured in this volume are just a small selection of the huge number and variety created by the Actresses' Franchise League (AFL) from 1908–14. Not only do they provide a fascinating glimpse into the popular theatrical styles of the period, but they also demonstrate the range of opinions, the struggles and the hopes of the Suffrage movement throughout those politically turbulent years. They are unapologetic propaganda pieces, written with passion and inspired by frustration. They are written to be heard, to communicate an idea and to provoke thought and inspire action. In performance these plays truly come alive and give performers and students interested in the period an opportunity to work with primary source material that illuminates theatrical styles, comic stereotypes and the role of theatre and entertainment in the agitation for female enfranchisement. This volume is a resource, therefore, for students, theatre professionals, teachers, researchers, historians and anyone interested in the journey of the long campaign for equal rights for women.

The AFL was founded in 1908, 'as a bond of union between all women in the Theatrical profession who are in sympathy with the Woman's Franchise Movement'. Membership was open to any woman who was or had been a professional actress, musician or music hall performer. The AFL was neutral with regard to tactics, stating in their constitution that they would 'assist all other Suffrage Societies and would work through educational methods such as Propaganda Meetings, Sale of Literature, Propaganda

Plays and Lectures to convince members of the Theatrical profession of the necessity to extend the franchise to women'.[2]

By 1914 membership had reached over 900, a Men's Group of actors, playwrights and other supporters connected with the theatre had been formed, and there were numerous Patrons of both sexes who, although not involved directly in the theatre, supported the AFL's work. The AFL worked closely with the Women Writers' Suffrage League (WWSL), also founded in 1908, and had many members from across the globe – notably the AFL's American-born President Gertrude Elliott and the Australian playwright and actress, Inez Bensusan, who ran the AFL Play Department. Prominent male supporters included George Bernard Shaw, Israel Zangwill, Laurence Housman, Lewis Casson and the actor-manager Johnston Forbes-Robertson. The dedicated actresses who founded the league remained members long after women were enfranchised, continuing to use the networks they had established to support theatrical charities and worthy causes. Minutes of an AFL meeting held on 15 January 1942 list three of the original members who by then were in their seventies – Decima Moore, Winifred Mayo and Eva Moore[3] – as present in addition to founder member and original Honorary Secretary of the League Adeline Bourne.[4]

The AFL and WWSL had a common cause to unite them; meaning that professional insecurities about sharing ideas could be laid aside, and that women's voices and creativity on stage and off were actively sought and encouraged. They were confident of purpose.

Elizabeth Robins, in her speech to the Women Writers at the Criterion in May 1911, said, 'Fellow-members of the League, you have such a field as never writers had before . . . You are, in respect of life described fearlessly from the woman's standpoint – you are in that position for which Chaucer has been so envied by his brother-poets, when they say he found the English language with the dew upon it. You find woman at the dawn . . . there she stands – the Real Girl! – waiting for you to do her justice.'[5]

Of course there has always been tremendous ambition among professional women in the theatre industry. They want to be creative and to show themselves as initiators rather than imitators

and have a desire both to see and be part of a more varied rep-
resentation of women on stage. Adeline Bourne, the Honorary
Secretary of the AFL, said, 'Never forget that Mrs. Pankhurst
and Christabel and Emmeline Pethick Lawrence never said they
were better than men. All they wanted [was] that they were as
good as men in every way.'[6] The AFL and WWSL allowed both
male and female playwrights to explore feminist themes overtly
and deliberately in a supportive environment and to 'compose
plays for performance safe from the limiting strictures of the
commercial theatre'.[7]

The plays in this collection will appeal to professional performers looking for monologues, duologues and one act plays
that are immediately playable and have a good variety of female
roles. Additionally, these plays are an invaluable resource for
teachers and students researching this period – providing specific primary source material into how the arguments for and
against the enfranchisement of women were presented in the
years preceding the First World War, and how the stereotypes of
suffragists and anti-suffragists were used for political and comic
effect theatrically. For both Drama and History sessions, the plays
are a useful tool for interactive work – short political pieces that
state the issues clearly whilst remaining in a dramatic context –
and help to open out discussions around the issue of women's
rights, the suffrage movement, representations of women in the
Edwardian period and different theatrical styles used for propaganda. The plays can and do stimulate debate and are a valuable
starting point for devising work, script and character develop-
ment. The opportunities for practical and theoretical design
work around the plays, the issues and the time period are also
extensive and their simple, flexible staging allows for a variety of
creative interpretations.

Neglecting the plays not only means the loss of their individual
merits as performance pieces and as a slice of theatrical history
but also a loss of a breadth of women's voices and experience.
It is only by staging these works – putting in the sort of time,
effort and energy that they were originally given – that justice to
them can be done, allowing audiences and performers to experience something of the passion and commitment that the original

performers and spectators felt. Those plays were a protest then. Now they can be a reminder, a celebration and an inspiration.

The Plays

How the Vote Was Won *by Cicely Hamilton and Christopher St John*
8F, 2M. RUNNING TIME APPROXIMATELY 45 MINUTES

How The Vote Was Won was and remains one of the most popular and well known suffrage plays. A brilliant ensemble piece, it is set in the living room of Horace and Ethel Cole in Brixton, London, on the day of a general women's strike called by Suffragettes because the Government has said that women do not need votes as they are all looked after by men. All the women who have previously supported themselves agree to leave their jobs and homes and instead insist on support from their nearest male relative. As Horace's female relatives arrive at his house one after the other, he comes to realize something must be done and rushes to Parliament, along with all the other men in London, to demand 'Votes for Women' as soon as possible.

First produced at the Royalty Theatre in London on 13 April 1909, *How the Vote Was Won* quickly became a favourite amongst suffrage audiences and was played all over the country with many different casts. Jane Comfort, a British actress and the niece of American playwright Madeline Lucette Ryley who was one of the Vice Presidents of the AFL, played Molly in the original cast and remembered famous music hall star Marie Lloyd appearing in one performance.[8] Reviews of the piece were glowing:

> It is the most rippling piece of fun which has been put on the boards for a long time, and the sooner it is put on for a regular run, the better for the public gaiety.. . . Why not an invitation performance for Cabinet Ministers? Cannot you imagine a nudge and a whisper creeping along their row of the stalls: 'I say, you fellows – we've been making fools of ourselves . . . Let's bring in a Bill.'[9]

It subsequently became popular with American suffragists and
was performed at a matinee in aid of The Equality League of
Self Supporting Women at Maxine Elliott's Theatre in New York
City on 31 March 1910 as part of a triple bill of British Suffrage
plays. AFL member Beatrice Forbes-Robertson played Winifred
and Fola La Follette, an American suffragist and actress, played
Ethel Cole.[10] Fola La Follette frequently performed a one-woman
version of the play at Suffrage meetings around the United
States, receiving a letter from Dr Anna Howard Shaw, President
of the National American Woman Suffrage Society which stated,
'I have wanted . . . to express to you . . . my appreciation of
the splendid help that play was to our cause . . . I approve of
the play, and think it would be of excellent service to any suffrage club.'[11] It was also produced at His Majesty's Theatre,
Johannesburg, by The Women's Reform Club in 1911 along with
Cicely Hamilton's other very popular suffrage work 'A Pageant
of Great Women'.[12]

Lady Geraldine's Speech *by Beatrice Harraden*
7F. RUNNING TIME APPROXIMATELY 20 MINUTES

Lady Geraldine's Speech is a fantastic, fun piece for actresses – Lady
Geraldine hasn't thought through the Suffrage cause and on a
visit to an old school friend meets some charismatic, successful
and intelligent women who soon enlighten and encourage her
onto the right path!

Published in 'Votes for Women' in April 1909 and performed at the WSPU (Women's Social and Political Union)
Women's Exhibition in Prince's Skating Rink, Knightsbridge
in May 1909 with Beatrice Forbes Robertson in the cast, *Lady
Geraldine's Speech* is an all-female ensemble piece, full of wonderfully eccentric Suffragette characters. Lady Geraldine bursts
into the drawing room of her school friend Dr Alice Romney
to ask for help in writing a speech to give to the National Anti-
Suffrage League, having apparently become rather high up in
the organization despite knowing nothing about it. Dr Alice, an
ardent Suffragette, eventually agrees to write the speech as a
favour and asks Lady Geraldine to wait. As she does, Dr Alice's
friends arrive for a Suffrage gathering – first a famous female

artist, then a Professor of Literature, then a famous pianist and finally a 'Votes for Women' newspaper seller. Lady Geraldine, impressed by the gathering, begins to realize through their conversation that they are all Suffragettes and have assumed she is too. Announcing herself as an Anti, she is defended by Dr Alice who then reads the speech she has written for her. The women are delighted with the absurdity of the arguments presented, and Lady Geraldine leaves having decided not to make the speech but to investigate the Suffrage movement instead. The whole play is delightful, representing Suffragettes as happy, talented, intelligent and good humoured and Lady Geraldine as misguided but charming. Beatrice Harraden defended the Suffragettes in response to criticism of the militant movement by feminist writer Sarah Grand, proudly writing of 'the good temper, the courage, the good camaraderie of the Suffragettes',[13] all of which are evident in the characters of Dr Alice's friends in *Lady Geraldine's Speech*. However because the characters are supporters of the WSPU, the play was not performed for other societies and was not published by the AFL, who had declared themselves neutral in relation to tactics and supporters of all the suffrage societies. Not all the women in the play have a voice – the maid has only one line and, unlike in many other suffrage plays, is not given a chance to express her opinion about the issues as the focus is on the exclusive set of educated, cultured women invited to the gathering. The speech that Dr Alice writes for Lady Geraldine is an interesting example of some contemporary anti-suffrage arguments, and the variety of pace and tone in the piece – Baillie's verse speaking and Crowninshield's piano playing – mean that the play, despite its short length, is a pleasure to both perform and watch.

Pot and Kettle *by Cicely Hamilton and Christopher St John*

3F, 2M. RUNNING TIME APPROXIMATELY 15 MINUTES

Pot and Kettle is a comic pleasure – a young woman returns to the bosom of her family in great distress having assaulted a suffragette who was sitting near her at an anti-suffragist meeting.

Pot and Kettle begins with Mr and Mrs Brewster at home, waiting for their daughter Marjorie who has been to an Anti-Suffrage meeting and excited that her being part of the Anti-Suffrage society will 'put her in the way of meeting some really nice people'. Marjorie's young man, Ernest is also waiting for her, as is her cousin Nell, a Suffragette. Marjorie eventually comes home, in floods of tears and reveals that she has been arrested for assaulting a Suffragette, Lady Susan Pengarvon, who was protesting at the meeting. Shocked at their daughter's behaviour, the Brewster's worries are alleviated by the surprise revelation that Nell became good friends with Lady Susan during a Suffragette protest at the Houses of Parliament. Nell resolves the situation over the telephone, much to the relief of a shaken Marjorie. *Pot and Kettle* is a very funny piece in which the audience is as surprised and intrigued as the characters in the play as to why Marjorie returns from the meeting so distressed and enjoys the playing out of the story.

Intriguingly, a note in the programme for the performance at the Scala Theatre states, 'The idea of this play was suggested to the Authors by an incident which occurred at a Meeting by the Anti-Suffrage League at Queen's Hall, in March 1909.'[14]

Miss Appleyard's Awakening *by Evelyn Glover*
3F. RUNNING TIME APPROXIMATELY 15 MINUTES

In *Miss Appleyard's Awakening*, an anti-suffrage campaigner collecting signatures for a petition finds herself in the home of a sympathizer but ends up inadvertently drawing her hostesses' attention to the contradictions in her arguments – and leaves having had quite the opposite effect to the one she intended.

Miss Appleyard's Awakening is a good, wordy duologue with clear characters and a well thought out presentation of the contradictions within Anti-Suffrage arguments. Having those arguments related by the character of Mrs Crabtree highlights their inadequacies and her increasingly frenzied attack on suffragists eventually makes Miss Appleyard think, seemingly for the first time about the her rights as a woman. The presentation of Miss Appleyard as an anti-suffragist is less obvious than that of Mrs Crabtree. The audience may have initially some sympathy with Miss Appleyard, a character who defines herself as an anti-suffragist and appears confident and independent, but as it becomes clear how little she has thought about the issues and how blind her own prejudice towards Suffragettes has been, she seems as blinkered as Mrs Crabtree in her own way. Fortunately Morton the maid is wiser, as in the way of most suffrage plays, and at the end it is she who will bring the newly awakened Miss Appleyard into the Suffrage fold. It has humour in the text – the initials ASS are neatly referenced – and in the playing and is a great piece to introduce an audience to the arguments surrounding the suffrage debate in this period. Evelyn Glover's most popular suffrage play 'A Chat with Mrs. Chicky' is also well worth seeking out.

Her Vote *by H. V. Esmond*

2F, 1M. RUNNING TIME APPROXIMATELY 15 MINUTES

Her Vote features a young suffragist whose plans to attend a political meeting are disrupted by an unexpected proposal from her young man. It is an unusual suffrage play as the character of the Girl, a suffragist, is portrayed rather more like that of an anti-suffragist. When questioned by the Clerk she is unable to elaborate on her views about the Suffrage and the issues surrounding it and instead responds by repeating words and phrases that she has heard but clearly doesn't really understand. Her firm resolve at the beginning of the piece to attend a Suffrage Meeting that night counts for nothing when a much more desirable offer arises. The actress and AFL member Eva Moore, who performed the role of the Girl in the first performance of *Her Vote*, recalled in her autobiography that the performance caused some controversy. 'I played the sketch, and it really was very funny. Two days later, at a meeting of the League, "someone" got up and stated that they had seen the sketch and that evidently "Eva Moore preferred Kisses to Votes", and suggested that I should be told not to play the sketch again, or resign.' Eva Moore did resign, temporarily, and recalls rejoining the League, 'reserving the right to myself to play in *any* play'.[15]

The character of the Drudge is a familiar one in suffrage comedy, a working class woman who has a better idea (although in this case, not a much better idea) about the potential impact of the vote on her life. The Clerk, tolerating the Girl's increasingly irritating presence in his office appears to have a clearer understanding of the issues than either of the other characters but, apart from a few well timed questions to the Girl, doesn't reveal his views on the matter. Written by Eva Moore's husband, the actor and playwright Henry Esmond, the play provides an interesting male viewpoint on the movement, criticizing the Girl for wanting to be part of a political movement without really knowing about it or understanding it – a criticism more often levelled at anti-suffragists in suffrage drama.

The Mother's Meeting *by Mrs Harlow Phibbs*

IF. RUNNING TIME APPROXIMATELY 5 MINUTES

While attending what she believes to be a Mothers Meeting Mrs Puckle finds herself having an unexpected reaction to what she hears.

A joyful, entertaining monologue, the piece uses a working class character to expose the inconsistencies in the Anti-Suffrage arguments. Interesting because it paints a picture of Mrs Puckle's home life and family; it also is another monologue directly spoken to the audience that allows for interaction between audience and performer. It can be tempting to see some of the comical misspellings and deliberate mispronunciations of words as patronizing or mocking the working class character; however it is more enjoyable to use them as a performer as possibilities for emphasis, to allow changes of tone, as an exaggerated accent guide and even perhaps to give a hint of Mrs Puckle sending her own way of talking up to amuse the audience. This piece also allows an actress free rein in inventing the way Mrs Puckle mimics the speech of Lady Clementina Pettigrew and other attendees at the meeting.

An Anti-Suffragist or The Other Side *by H. M. Paull*

IF. RUNNING TIME APPROXIMATELY 8 MINUTES

An Anti-Suffragist or The Other Side is a charming, clever monologue about a sheltered young woman who finds herself increasingly involved with her local Anti-Suffrage society and increasingly puzzled by what she learns there.

The slightly bewildered reciter is trying to convince the audience to join her local Anti-Suffrage Society by means of a thorough description of their last meeting. She has come from Little Pendleton, near Barchester – a plausible sounding but fictional conservative English middle class village in the countryside. The meeting she describes has an impressive list of influential speakers – an MP, an Archdeacon and an array of titled anti-suffragists who give an increasingly contradictory and nonsensical list of reasons why women do not and should not want the vote. The character of the reciter is disarmingly well-meaning and sincere, evidently uncomfortable with the way that women have been spoken about at the meeting but not confident about asserting her views over theirs, although she is clearly having some doubts about the facts and figures she is reporting to the audience.

This piece is a fantastic monologue for an actress, full of character, well written and enjoyable to play, as she is speaking directly to the audience. The Chairman's line before she starts is not crucial and can, if needed, be worked into the main speech as an introduction.

Tradition *by George Middleton*

2F, IM. RUNNING TIME APPROXIMATELY 20 MINUTES

Tradition is a thought-provoking piece about an actress visiting her parents and deals with their support for her career and their expectations of her future. Inspired by the suffragist and actress Fola La Follette's passion for acting and written by her husband, George Middleton, it is a quietly moving piece about family life, female aspiration and women's work. An unsuccessful but determined actress, Mary, returns home to see her parents. Her father expects her to give up and stay at home, but she is determined to follow her dreams of an acting career. When he discovers that Mary's mother has been supporting her financially through her own artistic endeavours, he decides to support her himself, dismissing his wife's evident pleasure in her work and role.

First performed at a matinee for the Woman Suffrage Party held at the Berkeley Theatre in New York City on Saturday, 24 January 1913, it was the third in a series of four short Suffrage plays. Middleton recalled in his memoirs that one of the other playwrights, Cleveland Moffett whose play *The Loser Wins* was also performed at that matinee, had written to him afterwards saying

> It is a very impressive piece of work, and interested
> Mrs. Moffett and myself so that we discussed it for about
> an hour after we returned home. The thought that you set
> forth has really influenced us in deciding certain points in the
> career of my little daughter.

Middleton was encouraged by an English critic, William Archer, to consider turning his one-act play into a full-length piece to develop the character of Mary's story more fully. Middleton did develop the idea and wrote a three-act play, *Nowadays*, which was booked to open in Washington in December 1913 with Fola La Follette in the part of the heroine, now called Diana rather than Mary. This production was postponed and eventually cancelled because it was suddenly not deemed to be a commercial proposition – however Middleton published the play that same year to great acclaim from suffragists and literary critics. The paper of the Woman Suffrage Party of New York, the 'Woman Voter', reviewed the published version of *Nowadays* as 'the first attempt by an American author to treat radically the economic phase of the woman question'. Keen to capture the zeitgeist, Middleton and La Follette performed readings of it throughout the country; he acting the male characters and she the female – but although productions were planned for both Chicago and New York, it was not produced. 'Here we had proof . . . that the play had audience appeal, had any one in the professional theatre been willing to give "Nowadays" a chance. But no one would.'[16]

Staging the Plays

All of the plays in this collection are easy to adapt to almost any
playing space, being set in one inside space – either a drawing
room or an office – and needing only a table and some chairs.
The original stage directions, costume and prop descriptions
give an indication of how the pieces were originally staged, but
the words are, of course, the most important part of any performance. Staging them fully with costumes and furniture and
exploring the details is a lot of fun for designers, performers and
audience members. Inspiration can certainly be drawn from
contemporary propaganda images depicting Suffragettes and
the changing fashions of the Edwardian era, and there are many
opportunities to play with the semiotics of class, taste and wealth
in these pieces.

If the decision is taken not to set a piece in the Edwardian
era, similarly influential modern references can be explored that
frame the piece for a present-day audience. This has the added
appeal of challenging preconceptions about dress and class in the
Edwardian era as well as those about Suffragettes, actresses and
feminists. In *How the Vote Was Won* and *Lady Geraldine's Speech*, the
arrival of Horace's relatives and Dr Alice's friends, all from different backgrounds and with different professions, provides a fantastic opportunity to research and explore women's fashions from
the period. Portraying the difference between an anti-suffragist
and a suffragist encourages reflection on visual representations
of women, both then and now. Mrs Crabtree in *Miss Appleyard's
Awakening*, Lady Geraldine and the reciter in *An Anti-Suffragist* are
all portrayals of anti-suffragists by suffrage writers. The idea of the
'womanly woman' and of 'feminine' dress and behaviour inform
these characters, and they probably look and behave very differently to Dr Alice's friends. The Girl in *Her Vote* may also share
some of the look of the anti-suffragists – she certainly does not
proudly show off her suffrage allegiance in her dress, unlike Mrs
Peter Puckle in *The Mothers' Meeting*, nor does she wear the colours
as some of Horace Cole's relatives do. Characters from the older
generation – such as the parents in *Pot and Kettle* and *Tradition* and
Aunt Lizzie in *How the Vote Was Won* – will also dress differently.

Of course, the plays in this collection do not need to be 'set' anywhere specific or in any specific historical period. Despite their particular focus on the issue of the enfranchisement of women, the themes and questioning of rights, roles and freedoms that run throughout the plays are relatable to many other eras, locations and cultures – both past and present. It is interesting to consider their effectiveness when presented with different cultural reference points in mind – and easy to explore this through rehearsal and performance. The use of language and the contemporary political references, for example in *Miss Appleyard's Awakening* can be trickier to transpose to another time or situation, but if the intention to communicate the ideas in the play is genuine, it is worthwhile and will be rewarding.

Many audiences and performers come to these plays with no knowledge of the suffrage movement at all, let alone the specific details and terminologies mentioned in the pieces. Presenting some of the plays in this volume together will help with creating reference points and bringing those reference points to life.

In *Miss Appleyard's Awakening*, Mrs Crabtree comes round with an anti-suffrage petition – something that is mentioned in *Lady Geraldine's Speech*, which in turn includes Dr Baillie mocking vacuous anti-suffragists and their uninformed political views – a theme that runs through *An Anti-Suffragist* and is turned against suffragists in *Her Vote*. Satirical descriptions of Anti-Suffrage meetings can be enjoyed in *An Anti-Suffragist, Pot and Kettle* and *The Mother's Meeting*, with only the first one not interrupted by protest from the floor. *How the Vote Was Won* and *Tradition* feature the male head of the household taking on a sympathetic view when the women in his life force him to confront the reality of their position within society.

The work of the AFL remains a little known but remarkable contribution to the campaign for Votes for Women. These plays give a glimpse into a turbulent time in women's history and an exciting period in women's writing and producing for the stage. Most of all, they are a delight to perform and watch, and I very much hope you enjoy them.

Notes

1   Julie Holledge, *Innocent Flowers: Women in the Edwardian Theatre*.
    London: Virago Press, 1981.
2   A. J. R., ed., *The Suffrage Annual and Women's Who's Who*. London:
    Stanley Paul, 1913.
3   'The Actresses' Franchise League' in *Votes for Women*, 24 December
    1908.
4   Actresses' Franchise League Minutes of Meeting, 15 January 1942.
5   Elizabeth Robins, 'The Women Writers', in *Way Stations*. New
    York: Dodd, Mead and Co., 1913.
6   Interview extract used in 'Suffragists and Suffragettes', *Eyewitness
    1900–1909*. BBC Audiobooks, 2004.
7   Sheila Stowell, *A Stage of Their Own: Feminist Playwrights of the
    Suffrage Era*. Ann Arbor: University of Michigan Press, 1992.
8   Quoted in Holledge, *Innocent Flowers*.
9   Review from *The New Age*, quoted in *How the Vote Was Won* by
    Cicely Hamilton and Christopher St John, Letchworth: Garden
    City Press, 1909.
10 Programme of matinee performance at Maxine Elliott's Theatre,
    New York City. 31 March 1910, Robinson Locke Collection, Billy
    Rose Theatre Division, New York Public Library.
11 *The Pittsburgh Press*, 25 September 1910.
12 Programme for performance at His Majesty's Theatre,
    Johannesburg, 1911. New York Public Library.
13 'Miss Beatrice Harraden's Defence of the Militant Methods', in
    Votes for Women, 2 July 1909.
14 Programme for performance at the Scala Theatre, London,
    12 November 1909.
15 Eva Moore, *Exits and Entrances*. London: Chapman and Hall, 1923.
16 George Middleton, *These Things Are Mine: The Autobiography of a
    Journeyman Playwright*. New York: Macmillan, 1947.

How the Vote Was Won

Cicely Hamilton and Christopher St John

1 Cicely Hamilton (1872–1952), member of the Actresses'
Franchise League and Women Writers' Suffrage League.
Photograph by Dover Street Studios, c.1910.

Cicely Hamilton 1872–1952

Born in London in 1872, Cicely Hamilton worked as an actress
before becoming a writer. Her first big success was *Diana of
Dobsons* (1908). Her works for the Suffrage movement include
A Pageant of Great Women (1909), *Jack and Jill and a Friend* (1911)
and her book *Marriage as a Trade* (1909). Hamilton also wrote

the lyrics for *March of the Women* and was a founding member of
the WWSL. Between 1914 and 1917 she worked at the Scottish
Women's Hospital in France and formed a repertory theatre
company at the Somme. After the First World War, Hamilton
worked as a freelance journalist and was a contributor to *Time
and Tide*. Other works include *William, an Englishman* (1918), *The
Child in Flanders* (1922), *The Old Vic* (1926) with Lilian Baylis and
her autobiography *Life Errant* (1935).

Christopher St John 1871–1960

Christopher St John, born Christabel Marshall in Exeter in
1871, changed her name after converting to Catholicism.
After studying at Somerville College, Oxford, she worked as a
secretary to Lady Randolph Churchill and met Edith Craig,
the daughter of Ellen Terry, in 1899. A member of both the
WWSL and the AFL, St John founded the Pioneer Players with
Craig in 1911. Her published works include *Hungerheart* (1915),
The Plays of Roswitha (1923), *Ellen Terry and Bernard Shaw: A
correspondence* (1931) and *Ethel Smyth, a biography* (1959).

First performed at the Royalty Theatre, London, on 13 April
1909 with the following cast:

Horace Cole (a clerk, about 30)	Mr Nigel Playfair
Ethel (his wife, 22)	Miss Athene Seyler
Winifred (her sister)	Miss Beatrice Forbes Robertson
Agatha Cole (Horace's sister)	Miss Winifred Mayo
Molly (his niece)	Miss Madeleine Roberts
Madame Christine (his distant relation)	Miss Maud Hoffman
Maudie Spark (his first cousin)	Miss Auriol Lee
Miss Lizzie Wilkins (his aunt)	Miss Helen Rous
Lily (his maid-of-all-work)	Miss Mignon Clifford
Gerald Williams (his neighbour)	Mr O. P. Heggie

First published by The Woman's Press in 1909.

Scene: *Sitting-room* in **Horace Cole's** *house at Brixton. The room is cheaply furnished in genteel style. The window looks out on a row of little houses, all of the Cole pattern. The door leads into a narrow passage communicating at once with the front door. The fireplace has a fancy mantel border, and over it is an overmantel, decorated with many photographs and cheap ornaments. The sideboard, a small bookcase, a table, and a comfortable armchair, are the chief articles of furniture. The whole effect is modest, and quite unpleasing.*

Time: *Late afternoon on a spring day in any year in the future.*

When the curtain rises, **Mrs Horace Cole [Ethel]** *is sitting in the comfortable armchair putting a button onto her husband's coat. She is a pretty, fluffy little woman who could never be bad-tempered, but might be fretful. At this minute she is smiling indulgently, and rather irritatingly, at her sister* **Winifred**, *who is sitting by the fire when the curtain rises, but gets up almost immediately to leave.* **Winifred** *is a tall and distinguished-looking young woman with a cheerful, capable manner and an emphatic diction which betrays the public speaker. She wears the colours of the NWSPU.*[1]

Winifred   Well, good-bye, Ethel. It's a pity you won't believe me. I wanted to let you and Horace down gently, or I shouldn't be here.

Ethel   But you're always prophesying these dreadful things, Winnie, and nothing ever happens. Do you remember the day when you tried to invade the House of Commons from submarine boats? Oh, Horace did laugh when he saw in the papers that you had all been landed on the Hovis wharf by mistake! 'By accident, on purpose!' Horace said. He couldn't stop laughing all the evening. 'What price your sister Winifred', he said. 'She asked for a vote, and they gave her bread.' He kept on – you can't think how funny he was about it!

Winifred   Oh, but I can! I know my dear brother-in-law's sense of humour is his strong point. Well, we must hope it will bear the strain that is going to be put on it today. Of course, when his female relations invade his house – all with the same story, 'I've come to be supported' – he may think it excruciatingly funny. One never knows.

Ethel   Winnie, you're only teasing me. They would never do such a thing. They must know we have only one spare bedroom, and that's to be for a paying guest when we can afford to furnish it.

Winifred   The servants' bedroom will be empty. Don't forget that all the domestic servants have joined the League and are going to strike, too.

Ethel   Not ours, Winnie. Martha is simply devoted to me, and poor little Lily *couldn't* leave. She has no home to go to. She would have to go to the workhouse.

Winifred   Exactly where she will go. All those women who have no male relatives, or are refused help by those they have, have instructions to go to the relieving officer. The number of female paupers who will pour through the workhouse gates tonight all over England will frighten the Guardians into blue fits.

Ethel   Horace says you'll never *frighten* the Government into giving you the vote.

Winifred   It's your husband, your dear Horace, and a million other dear Horaces who are going to do the frightening this time. By tomorrow, perhaps before, Horace will be marching to Westminster shouting out 'Votes for Women!'

Ethel   Winnie, how absurd you are! You know how often you've tried to convert Horace and failed. Is it likely that he will become a Suffragette just because –

Winifred   Just because – ? Go on, Ethel.

Ethel   Well, you know – all this you've been telling me about his relations coming here and asking him to support them. Of course I don't believe it. Agatha, for instance, would never dream of giving up her situation. But if they did come Horace would just tell them he *couldn't* keep them. How could he on £4 a week?

Winifred   How could he! That's the point! He couldn't, of course. That's why he'll want to get rid of them at any cost – even the cost of letting women have the Vote. That's why he and the majority of men in this country shouldn't for years have kept alive the foolish superstition that all women are supported by men. For years we have told them it was a delusion, but they could not take our arguments seriously. Their method of answering us was exactly that of the little boy in the street who cries 'Yah – Suffragette!' when he sees my ribbon.

Ethel   I always wish you wouldn't wear it when you come here . . . Horace does so dislike it. He thinks its unwomanly.

Winifred   Oh! does he? Tomorrow he may want to borrow it – when he and the others have had their object-lesson. They wouldn't listen to argument . . . so we had to expose their pious fraud about woman's place in the world in a very practical and sensible way. At this very minute working women of every grade in every part of England are ceasing work, and going to demand support and the necessities of life from their nearest male relatives, however distant the nearest relative may be. I hope, for your sake, Ethel, that Horace's relatives aren't an exacting lot!

Ethel   There wasn't a word about it in the *Daily Mail* this morning.

Winifred   Never mind. The evening papers will make up for it.

Ethel   What male relative are you going to, Winnie? Uncle Joseph?

Winifred   Oh, I'm in the fighting line, as usual, so our dear uncle will be spared. My work is with the great army of women who have no male belongings of any kind! I shall be busy till midnight marshalling them to the workhouse . . . This is perhaps the most important part of the strike. By this we shall hit men as ratepayers even when they have escaped us as relatives! Every man, either in a public capacity or a private one, will find himself face to face with the appalling problem of maintaining millions of women in idleness. Will the men take up the burden, d'ye think? Not they! (*looks at her watch.*) Good heavens! The strike began ages ago. I must be off. I've wasted too much time here already.

Ethel (*looking at the clock*)   I had no idea it was so late. I must see about Horace's tea. He may be home any minute.

Ethel *rings the bell.*

Winifred   Poor Horace!

Ethel (*annoyed*)   Why 'poor Horace'? I don't think he has anything to complain of.

Rings again.

Winifred   I feel some pity at this minute for all the men.

Ethel   What can have happened to Martha?

Winifred   She's gone, my dear, that's all.

Ethel   Nonsense. She's been with me ever since I was married, and I pay her very good wages.

*Enter **Lily,** a shabby little maid-of-all-work, dressed for walking, the chief effect of the toilette being a very cheap and very smart hat.*

Ethel   Where's Martha, Lily?

Lily   She's left, m'm.

Ethel   Left! She never gave me notice.

Lily   No, m'm, we wasn't to give no notice, but at three o'clock we was to quit.

Ethel   But why? Don't be a silly little girl. And you mustn't come in here in your hat.

Lily   I was just goin' when you rang. That's what I've got me 'at on for.

Ethel   Going! Where? It's not your afternoon out.

Lily   I'm goin' back to the Union. There's dozens of others goin' with me.

Ethel   But why –

Lily   Miss Christabel[2] – she told us. She says to us: 'Now look 'ere, all of yer – you who've got no men to go to on Thursday – yer've got to go to the Union', she says; 'and the one who 'angs back' – and she looked at me, she did – 'may be the person 'oo the 'ole strain of the movement is restin' on, the traitor 'oo's sailin' under the 'ostile flag', she says; and I says, 'That won't be me – not much!'

During this speech **Winifred** *puts on a sandwich board which bears the inscription: 'This way to the Workhouse.'*

Winifred   Well, Ethel, are you beginning to believe?

Ethel   Oh, I think it's very unkind – very wicked. How am I to get Horace anything to eat with no servants?

Winifred   Cheer up, my dear. Horace and the others can end the strike when they choose. But they're going to have a jolly bad time first. Good-bye.

Exit **Winnie**, *singing the 'Marseillaise'.*

Lily   Wait a bit, Miss. I'm comin' with yer (*sings the 'Marseillaise' too*)

Ethel   No, no. Oh, Lily, please don't go, or at any rate bring up the kettle first, and the chops, and the frying-pan. Please! Then I think I can manage.

Lily   (*coming back into the room and speaking impressively*) There's no ill-feeling. It's an objick lesson – that's all.

Exit **Lily**. **Ethel** *begins to cry weakly; then lays the table; gets bread, cruet, tea, cups, and the like, from the cupboard.* **Lily** *re-enters with a frying-pan, a kettle, and two raw chops.*

Lily   'Ere you are – it's the best I can do. You see, mum, I've got to be recognized by the State. I don't think I'm a criminal nor a lunatic, and I oughtn't to be treated as sich.

Ethel   You poor little simpleton. Do you suppose that, even if this absurd plan succeeds, *you* will get a vote?

Lily   I may – you never know your luck; but that's not why I'm giving up work. It's so as I shan't stop them as ought to 'ave it. The 'ole strain's on me, and I'm goin' to the Union – so good-bye, mum.

Exit **Lily.**

Ethel   And I've always been so kind to you! Oh, you little brute! What *will* Horace say? (*looking out of the window*). It can't be true. Everything looks the same as usual.

Horace's *voice is heard outside.*

Horace (*offstage*)   We must have at least sixteen Dreadnoughts this year.

Williams' *voice is heard outside.*

Williams (*offstage*)   You can't get 'em, old chap, unless you expect the blooming colonies to pay for 'em.

Ethel   Ah, here is Horace, and Gerald Williams with him. Oh, I hope Horace hasn't asked him to tea! (*She powders her nose at the glass, then pretends to be busy with the kettle.*)

Enter **Horace Cole** *– an English master in his own house – and* **Gerald Williams,** *a smug young man stiff with self-consciousness.*

Ethel   You're back early, aren't you, Horry? How do you do, Mr Williams?

Williams   How do you do, Mrs Cole? I just dropped in to fetch a book your husband's promised to lend me.

Horace *rummages in book-shelves.*

Ethel   Had a good day, Horry?

Horace   Oh, much as usual. Ah, here it is – (*reading out the title*) – 'Where's the Wash-tub now?' with a preface by Lord Curzon of Kedleston, published by the Men's League for Opposing Women's Suffrage. If that doesn't settle your missus, nothing will.

Ethel   Is Mrs Williams a Suffragette?

Williams   Rather; and whenever I say anything, all she can answer is, 'You know nothing about it.' Thank you, old man. I'll read it to her after tea. So long. Good-bye, Mrs Cole.

Ethel   Did Mrs Williams tell you anything this morning . . . before you went to the City?

Williams   About Votes for Women, do you mean? Oh, no. Not allowed at breakfast. In fact, not allowed at all. I tried to stop her going to these meetings where they fill the women's heads with all sorts of rubbish, and she said she'd give 'em up if I'd give up my footer matches; so we agreed to disagree. See you tomorrow, old chap. Good-bye, Mrs Cole.

Exit **Gerald Williams.**

Horace   You might have asked him to stop to tea. You made him very welcome – I don't think.

Ethel   I'm sorry; but I don't think he'd have stayed if I *had* asked him.

Horace   Very likely not, but one should always be hospitable. Tea ready?

Ethel   Not quite, dear. It will be in a minute.

Horace   What on earth is all this!

Ethel   Oh, nothing. I only thought I would cook your chop for you up here today – just for fun.

Horace   I really think, Ethel, that so long as we can afford a servant, it's rather unnecessary.

Ethel   You know you're always complaining of Martha's cooking. I thought you would like me to try.

Horace   My dear child! It's very nice of you. But why not cook in the kitchen? Raw meat in the sitting-room!

Ethel   Oh, Horry, don't!

She puts her arms round his neck and sobs. The chop at the end of the toasting fork in her hand dangles in his face.

Horace   What on earth's the matter? Ethel, dear, don't be hysterical. If you knew what it was to come home fagged to death and be worried like this.. . . I'll ring for Martha and tell her to take away these beastly chops. They're getting on my nerves.

Ethel   Martha's gone.

Horace   When? Why? Did you have a row? I suppose you had to give her a month's wages. I can't afford that sort of thing, you know.

Ethel (*sobbing*)   It's not you who afford it, anyhow. Don't I pay Martha out of my own money?

Horace   Do you call it ladylike to throw that in my face . . .

Ethel (*incoherently*)   I'm not throwing it in your face . . . but as it happens I didn't pay her anything. She went off without a word . . . and Lily's gone, too. (*She puts her head down on the table and cries.*)

Horace   Well, that's a good riddance. I'm sick of her dirty face and slovenly ways. If she ever does clean my boots, she makes them look worse than when I took them off. We must try and get a charwoman.

Ethel   We shan't be able to. Isn't it in the papers?

Horace   What *are* you talking about?

Ethel   Winifred said it would be in the evening papers.

Horace   Winifred! She's been here, has she? That accounts for everything. How that woman comes to be your sister I can't imagine. Of course she's mixed up with this wildcat scheme.

Ethel   Then you know about it!

Horace   Oh, I saw something about 'Suffragettes on Strike' on the posters on my way home. Who cares if they do strike? They're no use to anyone. Look at Winifred. What does she ever do except go round making speeches, and kicking up a row outside the House of Commons until she forces the police to arrest her. Then she goes to prison and poses as a martyr. Martyr! We all know she could go home at once if she would promise the magistrate to behave herself. What they ought to do is to try all these hysterical women privately and sentence them to be ducked – privately. Then they'd soon give up advertising themselves.

Ethel   Winnie has a splendid answer to that, but I forget what it is. Oh, Horry, was there anything on the posters about the nearest male relative?

Horace   Ethel, my dear, you haven't gone dotty, have you? When you have quite done with my chair, I – (*He helps her out of the chair and sits down.*) Thank you.

Ethel   Winnie said that not only are all the working women going to strike, but they are going to make their nearest male relatives support them.

Horace   Rot!

Ethel   I thought how dreadful it would be if Agatha came, or that cousin of yours on the stage whom you won't let me know, or your Aunt Lizzie! Martha and Lily have gone to *their* male relatives; at least, Lily's gone to the workhouse – it's all the same thing. Why shouldn't it be true? Oh, look, Horace, there's a cab – with luggage. Oh, what shall we do?

Horace   Don't fuss! It's stopping next door, not here at all.

Ethel   No, no; it's here. (*She rushes out.*)

Horace   (*calling after her*) Come back! You can't open the door yourself. It looks as if we didn't keep a servant.

Re-enter **Ethel,** *followed after a few seconds by* **Agatha. Agatha** *is a weary-looking woman of about 35. She wears the National Union colours,*[3] *and is dowdily dressed.*

Ethel   It *is* Agatha – and such a big box. Where *can* we put it?

Agatha (*mildly*)   How do you do, Horace. (*kisses him*) Dear
Ethel! (*kisses her*) You're not looking so well as usual. Would you
mind paying the cabman two shillings, Horace, and helping
him with my box? It's rather heavy, but then it contains all my
worldly belongings.

Horace   Agatha – you haven't lost your situation! You haven't
left the Lewises?

Agatha   Yes, Horace; I left at three o'clock.

Horace   My dear Agatha – I'm extremely sorry – but we
can't put you up here.

Agatha   Hadn't you better pay the cab? Two shillings so soon
becomes two-and-six.

Exit **Horace.**

Agatha   I am afraid my brother doesn't realize that I have
some claim on him.

Ethel   We thought you were so happy with the Lewises.

Agatha   So were the slaves in America when they had kind
masters. They didn't want to be free.

Ethel   Horace said you always had late dinner with them
when they had no company. Agatha. Oh, I have no complaint
against my late employers. In fact, I was sorry to inconvenience
them by leaving so suddenly. But I had a higher duty to perform
than my duty to them.

Ethel   I don't know what to do. It will worry Horace
dreadfully.

Re-enter **Horace.**

Horace   The cab *was* two-and-six, and I had to give a man
twopence to help me in with that Noah's ark. Now, Agatha,
what does this mean? Surely in your position it was very unwise
to leave the Lewises. You can't stay here. We must make some
arrangement.

Agatha   Any arrangement you like, dear, provided you support me.

Horace   I support you!

Agatha   As my nearest male relative, I think you are obliged to do so. If you refuse, I must go to the workhouse.

Horace   But why can't you support yourself? You've done it for years.

Agatha   Yes – ever since I was 18. Now I am going to give up work, until my work is recognized. Either my proper place is the home – the home provided for me by some dear father, brother, husband, cousin or uncle – or I am a self-supporting member of the State who ought not to be shut out from the rights of citizenship.

Horace   All this sounds as if you had become a Suffragette! Oh, Agatha, I always thought you were a lady.

Agatha   Yes, I *was* a lady – such a lady that at 18 I was thrown upon the world, penniless, with no training whatever which fitted me to earn my own living. When women become citizens I believe that daughters will be given the same chances as sons, and such a life as mine will be impossible.

Horace   Women are so illogical. What on earth has all this to do with your planting yourself on me in this inconsiderate way? You put me in a most unpleasant position. You must see, Agatha, that I haven't the means to support a sister as well as a wife. Couldn't you go to some friends until you find another situation?

Agatha   No, Horace. I'm going to stay with you.

Horace (*changing his tone and turning nasty*)   Oh, indeed! And for how long – if I may ask?

Agatha   Until the Bill for the removal of the sex disability is passed.

Horace (*impotently angry*)   Nonsense. I can't keep you, and I won't. I have always tried to do my duty by you. I think hardly

a week passes that I don't write to you. But now that you have
deliberately thrown up an excellent situation as a governess and
come here and threatened me – yes, threatened me – I think it's
time to say that, sister or no sister, I will be master in my own
house!

Enter **Molly,** *a good-looking young girl of about twenty. She is dressed
in well-cut, tailor-made clothes, wears a neat little hat, and carries some
golf-clubs and a few books.*

Molly   How are you, Uncle Horace? Is that Aunt Aggie? How
d'ye do? I haven't seen you since I was a kid.

Horace   Well, what have you come for?

Molly   There's a charming welcome to give your only niece!

Horace   You know perfectly well, Molly, that I disapprove of
you in every way. I hear – I have never read it, of course – but
I hear that you have written a most scandalous book. You live
in lodgings by yourself, when if you chose you could afford
some really nice and refined boarding-house. You have most
undesirable acquaintances, and altogether –

Molly   Cheer up, Uncle. Now's your chance of reforming me.
I've come to live with you. You can support me and improve me
at the same time.

Horace   I never heard such impertinence! I have always
understood from you that you earn more than I do.

Molly   Ah, yes; but you never *liked* my writing for money, did
you? You called me 'sexless' once because I said that as long as
I could support myself I didn't feel an irresistible temptation to
marry that awful little bounder Weekes.

Ethel   Reginald Weekes! How can you call him a bounder! He
was at Oxford.

Molly   Hullo, Auntie Ethel! I didn't notice you. You'll be glad
to hear I haven't brought much luggage – only a night-gown
and some golf-clubs.

Horace   I suppose this is a joke!

Molly   Well, of course that's one way of looking at it. I'm not going to support myself any longer. I'm going to be a perfect lady and depend on my Uncle Horace – my nearest male relative – for the necessities of life.

A motor horn is heard outside.

Molly   Aren't you glad that I am not going to write another scandalous book, or live in lodgings by myself!

Ethel (*at the window*)   Horace! Horace! There's someone getting out of a motor – a grand motor. Who can it be? And there's no one to answer the door.

Molly   That doesn't matter. I found it open, and left it open to save trouble.

Ethel   She's got luggage, too! The chauffeur's bringing in a dressing-case.

Horace   I'll turn her into the street – and the dressing-case, too.

He goes fussily to the door and meets **Madame Christine** *on the threshold. The lady is dressed smartly and tastefully. Age about forty, manners elegant, smile charming, speech resolute. She carries a jewel-case, and consults a legal document during her first remarks.*

Madame Christine   You are Mr Cole?

Horace   No! Certainly not! (*wavering*) At least, I was this morning, but –

Madame Christine   Horace Cole, son of John Hay Cole, formerly of Streatham, where he carried on the business of a –

A motor horn sounds outside.

Horace   I beg your pardon, but my late father's business has really nothing to do with this matter, and to a professional man it's rather trying to have these things raked up against him. Excuse me, but do you want your motor to go?

Madame Christine   It's not my motor any longer; and – yes, I do want it to go, for I may be staying here some time. I think you had one sister Agatha, and one brother Samuel, now dead. Samuel was much older than you –

Agatha   Why don't you answer, Horace? Yes, that's perfectly correct. I am Agatha.

Madame Christine   Oh, are you? How d'ye do?

Molly   And Samuel Cole was my father.

Madame Christine   I'm very glad to meet you. I didn't know I had such charming relations. Well, Mr Cole, my father was John Hay Cole's first cousin; so you, I think, are my second cousin, and my nearest male relative.

Horace (*distractedly*)   If anyone calls me that again I shall go mad.

Madame Christine   I am afraid you aren't quite pleased with the relationship!

Horace   You must excuse me – but I don't consider a second cousin exactly a relation.

Madame Christine   Oh, it answers the purpose. I suddenly find myself destitute, and I want you to support me. I am sure you would not like a Cole to go to the workhouse.

Horace   I don't care a damn where any of 'em go.

Ethel (*shocked*)   Horry! How can you!

Madame Christine   That's frank, at any rate; but I am sure, Cousin Horace, that in spite of your manners, your heart's in the right place. You won't refuse me board and lodging, until Parliament makes it possible for me to resume my work?

Horace   My dear madam, do you realize that my salary is £3 10s. a week – and that my house will hardly hold your luggage, much less you?

Madame Christine   Then you must agitate. Your female relatives have supported themselves up till now, and asked nothing from you. I myself, dear cousin, was, until this morning, running a profitable dressmaking business in Hanover Square. In my public capacity I am Madame Christine.

Molly I know! I've never been able to afford you.

Horace And do you think, Madame Christine –

Madame Christine Cousin Susan, please.

Horace Do you think that you are justified in coming to a poor clerk and asking him to support you – you could probably turn over my yearly income in a single week! Didn't you come here in your own motor?

Madame Christine At three o'clock that motor became the property of the Women's Social and Political Union. All the rest of my property and all available cash have been divided equally between the National Union and the Women's Freedom League. Money is the sinews of war, you know.

Horace Do you mean to tell me that you've given all your money to the Suffragettes! It's a pity you haven't a husband. He'd very soon stop your doing such foolish things.

Madame Christine I had a husband once. He liked me to do foolish things – for instance, to support him. After that unfortunate experience, Cousin Horace, you may imagine how glad I am to find a man who really is a man, and will support me instead. By the way, I should *so* much like some tea. Is the kettle boiling?

Ethel (*feebly*) There aren't enough cups! Oh, what *shall* I do?

Horace Never mind, Ethel; I shan't want any. I am going to dine in town and go to the theatre. I shall hope to find you all gone when I come back. If not, I shall send for the police.

Enter **Maudie Spark,** *a young woman with an aggressively cheerful manner, a voice raucous from much bellowing of music-hall songs, a hat of huge size, and a heart of gold.*

Spark 'Ullo! 'ullo! who's talking about the police? Not my dear cousin Horry!

Horace   How dare you come here?

Spark   Necessity, old dear. If I had a livelier male relative,
you may bet I'd have gone to him! But you, Horace, are the
only first cousin of this poor orphan. What are you in such a
hurry for?

Horace   Let me pass! I'm going to the theatre.

Spark   Silly jay! the theatres are all closed – and the halls
too. The actresses have gone on strike – resting indefinitely. I've
done my little bit towards that. They won't get any more work
out of Maudie Spark, Queen of Comédiennes, until the women
have got the vote. Ladies and fellow-relatives, you'll be pleased
to hear the strike's going fine. The big drapers can't open
tomorrow. One man can't fill the place of fifteen young ladies
at once, you see. The duchesses are out in the streets begging
people to come in and wash their kids. The City men are trying
to get taxi-men in to do their typewriting. Every man, like
Horry here, has his house full of females. Most of 'em thought,
like Horry, that they'd go to the theatre to escape. But there's
not a blessed theatre to go to! Oh, what a song it'll make. 'A
woman's place is the home – I don't think, I don't think, I don't
think.'

Horace   Even if this is not a plot against me personally, even
if there are other women in London at this minute disgracing
their sex –

Spark   Here stop it – come off it! If it comes to that, what are
you doing – threatening your womankind with the police and the
workhouse.

Horace   I was not addressing myself to you.

Agatha   Why not, Horace? She's your cousin. She needs your
protection just as much as we do.

Horace   I regard that woman as the skeleton in the cupboard
of a respectable family; but that's neither here nor there. I
address myself to the more lady-like portion of this gathering,
and I say that whatever is going on, the men will know what to

do, and will do it with dignity and firmness. (*The impressiveness of this statement is marred by the fact that* **Horace**'s *hand, in emphasizing it, comes down heavily on the loaf of bread on the table.*) A few exhibitions of this kind won't frighten them.

Spark   Oh, won't it! I like that! They're being so firm and so dignified that they're running down to the House of Commons like lunatics, and blackguarding the Government for not having given us the vote before!

Shouts outside of newsboys in the distance.

Molly   Splendid! Have they begun already?

Madame Christine   Get a paper, Cousin Horace. I know some men never believe anything till they see it in the paper.

Ethel   The boys are shouting out something now. Listen.

Shouts outside of Newsboys 'Extry special. Great strike of women. Women's strike. Theatres closed. Extry special edition. Star! News! 6.30 edition!'

Molly   You see. Since this morning Suffragettes have become women!

Ethel (*at window*)   Here, boy, paper!

Cries go on. 'Extry special Star. Men petition the Government. Votes for Women. Extry special.'

Ethel   Oh, heavens, here's Aunt Lizzie!

As **Ethel** *pronounces the name* **Horace** *dives under the table. Enter* **Aunt Lizzie** *leading a fat spaniel and carrying a birdcage with a parrot in it.* **Miss Elizabeth Wilkins** *is a comfortable, middle-aged body of a type well known to those who live in the less fashionable quarter of Bloomsbury. She looks as if she kept lodgers, and her looks do not belie her. She is not very well educated, but has a good deal of native intelligence. Her features are homely and her clothes about thirty years behind the times.*

Aunt Lizzie   Well, dears, all here? That's right. Where's Horace? Out? Just as well; we can talk more freely. I'm sorry

I'm late, but animals do so hate a move. It took a long time to make them understand the strike. But I think they will be very comfortable here. You love dogs, don't you, Ethel?

Ethel   Not Ponto. He always growls at me.

Aunt Lizzie   Clever dog! He knows you don't sympathize with the cause.

Ethel   But I do, Aunt; only I have always said that as I was happily married I thought it had very little to do with me.

Aunt Lizzie   You've changed your mind about that today, I should think! What a day it's been! We never expected everything would go so smoothly. They say the Bill's to be rushed through at once. No more broken promises, no more talking out; deeds, not words, at last! Seen the papers? The press are not boycotting us today, my dears. (**Madame Christine**, **Molly**, *and* **Maudie** *each take a paper.*) The boy who sold them to me put the money back into Ponto's collecting box. That dog must have made five pounds for the cause since this morning.

Horace (*puts his head out*)   Liar!

Molly   Oh, do listen to this. It's too splendid! (*reading from the paper*) 'Women's Strike – Latest: Messrs. Lyons and Co. announce that by special arrangement with the War Office the places of their defaulting waitresses will be filled by the non-commissioned officers and men of the 2nd Battalion Coldstream Guards. Business will therefore be carried on as usual.'

Madame Christine   What do you think of this? (*reading*) 'Latest Intelligence – It is understood that the Naval Volunteers have been approached by the authorities with the object of inducing them to act as charwomen to the House of Commons.'

Aunt Lizzie (*to* **Ethel**)   Well, my dear! Read, then, what the Star says.

Ethel (*tremulously reading*)   'The queue of women waiting for admission to Westminster workhouse is already a mile and a half in length. As the entire police force are occupied in dealing with the men's processions, Lord Esher has been approached with a view to ascertaining if the Territorials can be sworn in as special constables.'

Spark (*laughing*)   This is a little bit of all right. (*reading*) 'Our special representative, on calling upon the Prime Minister with the object of ascertaining his views on the situation, was informed that the Right Honourable gentleman was unable to receive him, as he was actively engaged in making his bed with the assistance of the boot-boy and a Foreign Office messenger.'

Aunt Lizzie   Always unwilling to receive people, you see! Well, he must be feeling sorry now that he never received us. Everyone's putting the blame on to him. It's extraordinary how many men – and newspapers, too – have suddenly found out that they have always been in favour of woman's suffrage! That's the sensible attitude, of course. It would be humiliating for them to confess that it was not until we held a pistol to their heads that they changed their minds. Well, at this minute I would rather be the man who has been our ally all along than the one who has been our enemy. It's not the popular thing to be an 'anti' any more. Any man who tries to oppose us today is likely to be slung up to the nearest lamp-post.

Ethel (*rushing wildly to the table*)   Oh, Horry! my Horry!

Horace *comes out from under the table.*

Aunt Lizzie   Why, bless the boy, what are you doing there?

Horace   Oh, nothing. I merely thought I might be less in the way here, that's all.

Aunt Lizzie   You didn't hide when I came in by any chance!

Horace   I hide from you! Aren't you always welcome in this house?

Aunt Lizzie   Well, I haven't noticed it particularly; and I'm not calling today, you understand, I've come to stay.

Horace, *dashed and beaten, begins to walk up and down the room, and consults* **Ethel.**

Aunt Lizzie   Well, well! I won't deny it was a wrench to leave 118a, Upper Montagu Place, where I've done my best for boarders, old and young, gents and ladies, for twenty-five years – and no complaints! A home from home, they call it. All my ladies had left before I started out, on the same business as all of us – but what those poor boys will do for their dinner tonight I don't know. They're a helpless lot! Well, it's all over; I've given up my boarding-house, and I depend on you, Horace, to keep me until I am admitted to citizenship. It may take a long time.

Horace   It must *not* take a long time. I shan't allow it. It shall be done at once. Well, you needn't all look so surprised. I know I've been against it, but I didn't realize things. I thought only a few howling dervishes wanted the vote; but when I find that you – Aunt – Fancy a woman of your firmness of character, one who has always been so careful with her money, being declared incapable of voting! The thing is absurd.

Spark   Bravo! Our Horry's waking up.

Horace (*looking at her scornfully*)   If there are a few women here and there who *are* incapable – I mention no names, mind – it doesn't affect the position. What's going to be done? Who's going to do it? If this rotten Government think we're going to maintain millions of women in idleness just because they don't like the idea of my Aunt Lizzie making a scratch on a bit of paper and shoving it into a ballot-box once every five years, this Government have reckoned without the men – (*General cheering*) I'll show 'em what I've got a vote for! What do they expect? You can't all marry. There aren't enough men to go round, and if you're earning your own living and paying taxes you ought to have a say; it's only fair. (*General cheering and a specially emphatic* 'Hear, hear' *from* **Madame Christine**) The Government are narrow-minded idiots!

Madame Christine   Hear! hear!

Horace   They talk as if all the women ought to stay at home washing and ironing. Well, before a woman has a wash-tub, she must have a home to put it in, mustn't she? And who's going to give it her? I'd like them to tell me that. Do they expect *me* to do it?

Agatha   Yes, dear.

Horace   I say if she can do it herself and keep herself, so much the better for everyone. Anyhow, who are the Government? They're only representing *me*, and being paid thousands a year by *me* for carrying out *my* wishes.

Molly   Oh, er – what ho!

Horace (*turns on her angrily*)   I like a woman to be a woman – that's the way I was brought up; but if she insists on having a vote – and apparently she does

All   She does! She does!

Horace   I don't see why she shouldn't have it. Many a woman came in here at the last election and tried to wheedle me into voting for her particular candidate. If she has time to do that – and I never heard the member say then that she ought to be at home washing the baby – I don't see why she hasn't time to vote. It's never taken up much of *my* time, or interfered with *my* work. I've only voted once in my life – but that's neither here nor there. I know what the vote does for me. It gives me a status; that's what you women want – a status.

All   Yes, yes; a status

Horace   I might even call it a *locus standi*. If I go now and tell these rotten Cabinet Ministers what I think of them, it's my *locus standi* –

Maudie   That's a good word

Horace   – that will force them to listen to me. Oh, I know. And, by gum! I'll give them a bit of my mind. They shall hear a few home truths for once. 'Gentlemen', I shall say – well, that won't be true of all of them to start with, but one must give

'em the benefit of the doubt – 'gentlemen, the men of England
are sick and tired of your policy. Who's driven the women
of England into this? *You* – (*he turns round on* **Ethel**, *who jumps
violently*) – because you were too stupid to know that they meant
business – because you couldn't read the writing on the wall.
(*Hear, hear!*) It may be nothing to you, gentlemen, that every
industry in this country is paralyzed and every Englishman's
home turned into a howling wilderness –

Molly   Draw it mild, Uncle.

Horace   A howling wilderness, I repeat – by your refusal to
see what's as plain as the nose on your face; but I would have
you know, gentlemen, that it *is* something to us. We aren't slaves.
We never will be slaves –

Agatha   Never, never!

Horace   – and we insist on reform. Gentlemen, conditions
have changed, and women have to work. Don't men encourage
them to work, *invite* them to work?

Agatha *Make* them work.

Horace   And women are placed in the battle of life on the
same terms as we are, short of one thing, the *locus standi* of a
vote.

Maudie   Good old *locus standi!*

Horace   If you aren't going to give it them, gentlemen, and
if they won't go back to their occupations without it, we ask
you, how they're going to live? Who's going to support them?
Perhaps you're thinking of giving them all old age pensions
and asking the country to pay the piper! The country will see
you damned first, if, gentlemen, you'll pardon the expression.
It's dawning upon us all that the women would never have
taken such a step as this if they hadn't been the victims of gross
injustice.

All   Never.

Horace   Why shouldn't they have a voice in the laws which regulate the price of food and clothes? Don't they pay for their food and clothes?

Maudie   Paid for mine since the age of six.

Horace   Why shouldn't they have a voice in the rate of wages and the hours of labour in certain industries? Aren't they working at those industries? If you had a particle of common sense or decent feeling, gentlemen'

Enter **Gerald Williams.** *He shouts incoherently and in a hoarse voice. He is utterly transformed from the meek, smug being of before. He is wearing several ribbons and badges and carrying a banner bearing this inscription: 'The men of Brixton demand votes for women this evening.'*

Williams   Cole! Cole! Come on! come on! You'll be late. The procession's forming up at the town hall. There's no time to lose. What are you slacking here for? Perhaps this isn't good enough for you. I've got twelve of them in my drawing-room. We shall be late for the procession if we don't start at once. Hurry up! Come on! Votes for Women! Where's your banner? Where's your badge? Down with the Government! Rule Britannia! Votes for Women! D'you want to support a dozen women for the rest of your life, or don't you? Every man in Brixton is going to Westminster. Borrow a ribbon and come along. Hurry up, now! Hooray! (*rushes madly out crying* 'Votes for Women! Rule Britannia; Women, never, never shall be slaves! Votes for Women!')

All the women who are wearing ribbons decorate **Horace.**

Ethel   My hero!

She throws her arms round him.

Horace   You may depend on me – all of you – to see justice done. When you want a thing done, get a man to do it! Votes for Women!

Agatha   *gives him a flag which he waves triumphantly.*

Horace   *marches majestically out of the door, with the women cheering him enthusiastically.*

CURTAIN

Notes

1 The colours of the WSPU (Women's Social and Political Union)
   were purple, white and green.
2 A reference to Christabel Pankhurst, one of the leaders of the
   WSPU.
3 The colours of the NUWSS (National Union of Women's Suffrage
   Societies) were red, white and green.

Lady Geraldine's Speech

Beatrice Harraden

2 Beatrice Harraden (1864–1936), a member of the WSPU,
the Women Writers' Suffrage League and the London Graduates'
Suffrage Society. Photograph by Bain Studios, 1913.
Courtesy of Library of Congress, Prints & Photographs Division.

Beatrice Harraden 1864–1936

Born in London in 1864, Beatrice Harraden was educated at Cheltenham Ladies College, Queen's College and Bedford College and graduated from London University with a BA in Arts, having studied Greek, Latin and English Literature. An ardent Suffragist, she was a member of the WSPU, the WWSL and the London Graduates' Suffrage Society. She was most well-known for writing novels and articles. Her publications include *Ships that Pass in the Night* (1894), *Katherine Frensham* (1903), *The Scholar's Daughter* (1906), *Interplay* (1908) and *Out of the Wreck I Rise* (1912). Plays include *The Outcast* (1909) written with Bessie Hatton and *The Traveller and the Temple of Knowledge* (1911).

Characters

Dr Alice Romney – A Medical Woman
Lady Geraldine Boleyn – Dr Alice Romney's School Friend
Miss Gertrude Silberthwaite – An Eminent Artist
Miss Nora Baillie – A Prof. of Literature
Miss Hilda Crowninshield – A Famous Pianist
Miss Nellie Grant – A Typist and Shorthand Writer
Jane – A Maid

Lady Geraldine's Speech was first performed at the WSPU Women's Exhibition in the Prince's Skating Rink, Knightsbridge on 15 May 1909.

It was first published in the WSPU newspaper 'Votes for Women' on 2 April 1909.

Scene: Dr Alice Romney's *drawing room in Nottingham Place. It is her fortnightly Suffrage At Home day. She is seated at her writing desk near the window. She is of middle stature, and has a strong, capable face.*

Enter **Maid** *with card.*

Maid A lady asks specially to see you. I said you were engaged until three o'clock. But she insisted.

Dr Alice (*looking at the card and smiling*) Show her in, Jane.

Enter, hurriedly, shown in by maid, the **Lady Geraldine Boleyn.**

Lady Geraldine Oh, my dear, how good of you to see me. I hope I am not interrupting any operation. Not that I suppose you do perform operations in drawing rooms! But I had to see you instantly, whatever you were doing. I've dashed up purposely from Eastbourne. The fact is, Alice, I've got myself into a most awful hole. You'll help me out, won't you? You always have helped me out of my difficulties. Nothing more than you ought to have done, considering how I used to come to your rescue over your French compositions in the dear old Cheltenham College days. My word, you were bad at French, weren't you?

Dr Alice (*nodding*) Yes. And I'm not much better now. Languages were always a trial to me. I used to think you were a perfect wonder at them.

Lady Geraldine So I was. So I am still. Don't let there be any mistake about that! Well now, to business. As I told you, I've got myself into a most fearful scrape. The worst in my life – absolutely the worst.

Dr Alice (*reproachfully*) Geraldine, Geraldine, what on earth have you been up to? Are you never going to learn discretion?

Lady Geraldine Apparently never. There's no doubt that I have committed a terrible indiscretion. I've compromised myself with – well, I hardly like to tell you – with – the Women's National Anti-Suffrage League.

Dr Alice (*brightening up*)   Is that all?

Lady Geraldine   Isn't it enough, in all conscience? I'm at my wits' end. I haven't slept for nights, for years. Look how drawn my face is. If I'm not careful, I shall begin to look clever. Yes, I've got into the toils of the National Anti-Suffrage League. I've been made into a president or vice-president, or honorary secretary, or supporter, or something of the sort, and I have to take the chair at a large meeting at the Imperial Hall next week and make a speech, and use all the anti-suffrage arguments on this wretched sheet of paper – oh, where is it? (*looking for it in her muff and satchel*) Ah, here it is. It's like a nightmare to me. Every time I try and look at it, all the letters seem to chase each other off the paper, and there's only a blank left – like my brain. If you won't help me, I shall perish. I know I shall.

Dr Alice   But my dear Geraldine, I'm a Suffragist, a Suffragette, a militant. You've come to the wrong person.

Lady Geraldine (*coaxingly*)   I've come to my old school chum. As if being a Suffragist or an Anti-Suffragist could make any difference to that eternal fact.

Dr Alice (*laughing*)   No, you're right! Well, what do you want me to do?

Lady Geraldine   I want you to write my speech for me, and coach me up in it. There! Don't look so disagreeable. You're so handsome when you're pleasant. And so hideous when you're cross. Ah, that's better. Now, here are some of the arguments. As I told you, I tried to glance at them, but failed. So I haven't really gone into details. I haven't really gone into the matter at all, between you and me. But (*suddenly recollecting herself*) I felt strongly, on general lines, that it was impossible for me to take the responsibility of being in favour of Woman's Suffrage.

Dr Alice   How well you roll those words out! Someone has made you learn that sentence by heart. (*Repeats it*) 'But I felt strongly, on general lines, that it was impossible for me to take the responsibility of being in favour of Woman's Suffrage.' I must say I wonder you dare take the still greater responsibility of being against it.

Lady Geraldine (*waving her hand in dismissal of Dr Alice's remark*)   Come now, Alice. Do begin. We're wasting time. Allow me to conduct you to your desk. Here's paper. And here's your stylo. And here am I waiting on you as usual. Oh, you can make as much fun of me as you like, and lecture me as much as you like. I was always good tempered, wasn't I? I don't mind what you say to me, as long as you help me with my speech.

Dr Alice   Why don't you go and get an Anti-Suffragist friend to do this for you?

Lady Geraldine   My dear girl, don't be ridiculous. With a few notable exceptions, all the Anti-Suffragists have my sort of brains. How can we possibly help each other? Do begin. I'm losing patience with you.

Dr Alice   But you have heaps of splendid men amongst you. Go to them.

Lady Geraldine   Certainly not! It's one thing to sing small about your sex, but quite another thing to sing small about yourself – except to a dear old school chum who used to be a regular old brick, but who evidently isn't one any longer (*plaintively*). I never dreamed that you would fail me. What on earth shall I do? I shall make an awful fiasco, and disgrace myself and my Cause, and it will be your fault. You wouldn't wish to see me humiliated, would you? And surely you wouldn't wish my Cause to be disgraced. You've always said Causes saved one. Those have been your very words, Alice. Causes saved one, it did not matter what they were.

Dr Alice (*laughing*)   Nothing could ever save you. You're spoilt through and through. Here, give me the precious arguments. Sit down by the fire, and don't chatter for a minute or two, and I'll see what I can do for you.

Lady Geraldine (*taking up her skirt and dancing round a little*)   A-ha! I knew she would come round. These grim people are always the easiest to deal with. Be sure and write clearly, dear. I never could read your handwriting.

She dances into a chair and sits primly up, twiddling her fingers. A pause.

Dr Alice   I think you might begin in this way: 'Ladies and gentlemen, I am here tonight to explain to you some of the weighty reasons which have decided me, after much anxious thought and study, to become a determined opponent of Woman's Suffrage.'

Lady Geraldine   Excellent! Sounds as if I'd studied the question for untold centuries, doesn't it?

Dr Alice   Then I think you'd better touch at once on the 'unwomanliness' of the whole movement, and the danger to the home. And you might enlarge on the 'harem' theme.

Lady Geraldine   The harem theme? What's that? I don't remember that on the list. Not that I remember anything.

Dr Alice   It is not called that. It's called, 'The immense indirect influence now possessed by women.' To me, personally, a most degrading influence. After that you might beat the Imperial Drum.

Lady Geraldine   The Imperial –

The door opens. Enter, unannounced, **Miss Gertrude Silberthwaite***, an eminent artist. She is charmingly dressed, and has an engaging personality.*

Silberthwaite   Ah, busy, I see, Dr Alice. I'm rather early. Shall I go away and come back in half-an-hour or so?

Dr Alice   No, no. Sit down by the fire with my friend – an old school friend. I'm throwing together a speech for her. She's a new hand. I don't mind you talking so long as you don't talk to me.

Lady Geraldine *and* **Gertrude Silberthwaite,** *who have already greeted, settle down together.*

Silberthwaite   Dr Alice has a most enviable gift of concentration. She can study the most abstruse subject under any conditions whatsoever. So she is helping you with your first speech? Well, you couldn't have anyone better to help you. She's so splendid at arranging the arguments in their most forceful fashion. Shall you be nervous?

Lady Geraldine (*uneasily*)   Yes.

Silberthwaite   Ah, well, we all have to go through that. But it's worth while for the sake of the Cause, isn't it?

Lady Geraldine (*doubtfully*)   Yes.

Silberthwaite   I'm just painting Dr Alice's portrait. A difficult face. So handsome when she's pleasant! And so ugly when she's disagreeable.

Lady Geraldine (*delighted*)   That's exactly what I say. My very words a few minutes ago! Then you are an artist – a portrait painter? May I ask your name? I'm so interested in pictures.

Silberthwaite   Silberthwaite.

Lady Geraldine (*enraptured*)   Gertrude Silberthwaite! You don't mean it. I am proud and delighted to see you. I've always wanted to meet you. But one never comes across you anywhere. I always heard you were a recluse.

Silberthwaite (*smiling*)   I'm not by nature a society-bird. And moreover I haven't much spare time – none, in fact. But the Suffrage Movement has brought all us professional women out of our libraries and studios and all our other hiding places. We had to take our share in it, or else be ashamed of ourselves. I really do think it is a wonderful movement, don't you? And quite apart from anything to do with the vote itself, it is so splendid coming in intimate contact with a lot of fine women all following different professions or businesses. That's one of our advantages over the Anti-Suffragists, isn't it? They have no means of understanding personally the inner meaning of the whole Movement. I'm sorry for them, aren't you?

Lady Geraldine (*fervently*)   Yes, for some of them.

Silberthwaite   Do you know I'm planning to paint
a Suffrage Picture for next year's Academy, a group of
representative Suffragist Women. Ellen Terry for the Drama,
Mrs Garrett Anderson for Medicine, Mrs Ayrton for Science,
Miss Elizabeth Robins for literature, Christabel Pankhurst for
Politics, and –

Enter **Miss Nora Baillie** *a Professor of Literature and a brilliant
lecturer. She is particularly fresh-looking and has a fine enthusiastic face,
with eyes far apart.*

Baillie (*gaily*)   What, Dr Alice, busy making out prescriptions?
Ah no, I see you haven't the prescription look on your face! A
letter to the Prime Minister perhaps! A love letter to the Home
Secretary! A valentine to the Governor of Holloway! Who can
tell? Anything may happen in these days.

Silberthwaite (*laughing and beckoning to* **Baillie**):   Don't talk
to her, Miss Baillie. She's concocting a speech. Come and talk to
us instead. You do look in splendid form this afternoon. What
have you been doing?

Baillie   I've just given the best Chaucer lecture I've ever
given in my life. And the class was magnificent. Heavens, what
a difference it makes when you know you have you class with
you!

Lady Geraldine   Chaucer! How interesting! I haven't heard
his name mentioned since I was at school. Do tell me something
about him!

Baillie (*quoting with animation*):

'His stature was not very tall.
Leane he was, his legs were small.
Hosed within a stock of red.
A buttoned bonnet on his head.
His beard was white, trimmed round.
His countenance blithe and merry found.'

I wonder whether Chaucer would have conceded us the vote.
I have my doubts. But I have no doubt about Shakespeare.
None. I can't conceive it possible that he who gave us Portia,
Hermione, Cordelia, Rosalind, Beatrice, Imogen and all his
other splendid women of brain, education and initiative, would
have withheld us grudgingly the rights of full citizenship. I
intend to die in the belief that he would have been on our side.
I'm sure he's on the platform at all Suffrage Meetings calling
out inaudibly: 'Votes for Women!' (*Turning to Lady Geraldine*):
Don't you agree with me?

Lady Geraldine (*shyly*)   I've never thought of it.

Silberthwaite   Nor have I. But I daresay she's right.

Baillie   Of course I'm right! What a pity the Prime Minister
hasn't Shakespeare's mind! There's no denying he hasn't, is
there? (*to* **Lady Geraldine**)

Lady Geraldine (*pensively*)   I suppose there isn't.

Silberthwaite   (*gaily*)   You appear to be in some doubt.

Lady Geraldine (*laughing*)   Oh no, not about that! But I was
just wondering –

Enter **Miss Hilda Crowninshield,** *a famous pianist.*

Silberthwaite   Ah, here's Hilda Crowninshield. Hurrah!

Crowninshield (*greeting them all*)   Here I am. Just back from
a concert at Manchester. Good afternoon, Dr Alice. Busy, I see.
(*Turning to* **Silberthwaite**) What is she doing? Shall I disturb
her if I try the piano?

Baillie   Oh! dear no. She's only writing a speech. As long
as you don't talk to her, you may introduce the whole of the
Queen's Hall Orchestra into this room, and she won't turn a
hair.

Crowninshield   Good. I want to run through the two little
Brahms pieces I promised to play this afternoon. If the piano is
very much out of tune, and there are more than five or six notes
broken, I shall have to choose some other things, that's all!

She sits down at the piano. **Lady Geraldine,** *who has been exceedingly stirred by her arrival, goes up to her.*

Lady Geraldine (*excitedly*)   Miss Crowninshield, I must speak to you. I cannot tell you what your playing means to me. I'd rather hear you than anyone in the world! I don't know what you do to me. When I hear you play, I feel myself capable of everything great and good.

Crowninshield (*greatly pleased, and touching her gently on the hand*)   Thank you. Then you must be passionately fond of music?

Lady Geraldine   Passionately. It is the language I understand.

Crowninshield (*beginning to touch the notes*)   Ah, not so bad! And I declare Dr Alice has had it tuned! I never expected such luck. Yes, I can play one or two of Brahms's Intermezzi, and perhaps a Chopin waltz. Perhaps even a bit of Grieg. (*She addresses herself to* **Lady Geraldine**) Yes?

Lady Geraldine (*delighted*)   Yes, yes! How good of you to come and play at Dr Alice's.

Crowninshield   Good? Why, I love playing to my Suffrage comrades. I'd do anything for them! Play the trombone, if they wanted it fearfully!

She begins Brahm's First Intermezzo. After she has been playing for a little while, enter **Nellie Grant,** *a typist and shorthand writer. She carries, slung over her shoulder, a bag with one remaining copy of* Votes for Women. *She looks extremely fatigued.* **Hilda Crowninshield** *glances up and leaves off playing and joins the others.*

Crowninshield   Why, my dear child, you look worn out. Thoroughly at the end of yourself. Let's ring for tea for her immediately. (*They ring for tea.*)

Nellie Grant   Tired, but very proud, Miss Crowninshield. I've had a most successful day. Sold all my Votes for Women except one solitary copy, and had some useful little talks with lots of people. One man bought six copies. He said he had been an Anti until yesterday, when he went to an Anti meeting and that converted him! (*Laughter.*)

Crowninshield   Bravo! (*Runs to the piano and plays a few bars of the waltz from 'The Merry Widow'. They laugh, clap, and dance a little.*)

Baillie   I really do think the Antis are our best friends.

Lady Geraldine   Why? I don't quite understand. I should have thought they were very formidable foes.

Silberthwaite   Oh dear no! You needn't have any fears about that. You see, with a few exceptions, they can't speak – they haven't had the practice – they haven't learnt how to hold an audience.

Lady Geraldine   But when they have learnt, what then?

Baillie   Even then they can't be formidable. Remember for your comfort, they haven't got an irresistible champion as we have.

Lady Geraldine (*entirely mystified*)   An irresistible champion?

Crowninshield   She means the Spirit of the Age.

Lady Geraldine (*smiling blankly*)   The Spirit of the Age?

Baillie   And lots of them haven't 'gone into it'! I know they haven't. One of them brought me the Anti-Suffrage Petition to sign, and told me quite frankly, when I advanced some arguments in favour of Woman's Suffrage, that she had not 'gone into it', but that she wanted to get as many signatures as quickly as possible for that petition which was sent in yesterday, you know – 7 miles long or 7 feet high – I forget which! They may get signatures – whole villages of signatures – but they can't really hope to influence people if they haven't taken the trouble to influence themselves, can they?

Lady Geraldine (*uncomfortably*)   No.

Silberthwaite   Don't give them one anxious thought. They'll soon 'fold their tents, like the Arabs, and as silently steal away'!

Crowninshield *who is still at the piano, improvises and sings softly*)

'The night shall be filled with music, and
the cares which beset the day.
Shall fold their tents, like the Arabs, and
as silently steal away.'

Tea is brought in.

Lady Geraldine (*who has been slowly gathering herself together for a declaration of faith*)   I have something to tell you all. You've been taking it for granted that I'm a Suffragist. Well, I'm not. I'm an Anti-Suffragist.

Silberthwaite   Great heavens! How delightful! I've been longing to meet one face to face. No one brought me the Anti-Suffrage Petition.

Baillie   Do tell us your name. Who are you?

Lady Geraldine   Geraldine Boleyn.

Baillie (*turning to the others*)   Why, of course! Lady Geraldine Boleyn. She's going to take the chair on the 15th at the Imperial Hall. Surely I'm not mistaken.

Lady Geraldine (*frankly*)   Yes, that's quite right. And as I couldn't manage my speech, I came to my old school friend in my distress. I know it sounds absurd, but it's true.

Dr Alice (*looking up for the first time from her desk*)   Idiot! Why did you give yourself away? I could shake you.

Lady Geraldine   Alice, I simply couldn't have held out for a moment longer. I couldn't have gone on pretending by my silence that I was one of them.

Dr Alice (*getting up from her desk, and turning fiercely to her comrades*)   You mustn't betray her. I wouldn't have her betrayed for worlds. She's very dear to me. She has always been wonderfully good to me, though she has been a great nuisance at times and has given me a lot of trouble, and has always made the most unreasonable demands on me – and – well – I've liked it. She's my oldest and dearest school friend, and we plotted all sorts of mischief together in the happy old days. And if that isn't a Sacred bond, then nothing is. Nearly all the pleasures I had in my holidays came through her – I should never have known all the sweet pleasures of the country but for her – joys which abide with one for ever, when other things have passed out of one's life. I can't and won't have her humiliated. If I hadn't helped her over her speech, she would have probably made herself ridiculous – and I couldn't have stood that – I had to help her – and I shall always have to help her – if she becomes an anarchist and takes the chair at an anarchist meeting I shall have to write her speech for that too. I . . . (*She breaks off suddenly*) Promise me you won't give her away.

All Four   Of course. Our word of honour.

They all stretch out their hands to **Lady Geraldine** *and make a charming group around her.*

Baillie (*gaily*)   There's nothing, however, in our oath to prevent us from laughing a little, is there? Oh, and to think I shan't be able to go and heckle you! I can't heckle Dr Alice's old school friend. And I'd bought a ticket surreptitiously and with the utmost difficulty!

Silberthwaite   As I told you, I've never seen a real Anti-Suffragist before. Do let me paint your portrait! Side face would be best, I think. I'm not quite sure though. No it must be full face. Yes, full face.

Nellie Grant   Do tell me if it's true that there's going to be a 'No Votes for Women' paper, with a Union Jack on the cover. I shall be jealous.

Crowninshield (*taking* **Lady Geraldine's** *arm*):   Don't you dare tease her any more! Votes or no votes, she and I speak the same language, don't we?

Dr Alice   Well, now for the speech, Geraldine. I've quite enjoyed this little job. I'm rather pleased with it. I think I've brought in all the points. Degradation of Womanhood. Degradation and disintegration of entire Empire. Dominant female vote in all matters concerning the Army and Navy, our relations with foreign Powers, with our Colonies, and with India. Physical force argument. Women have to safeguard the past and the future, and it is the men's work to look after the present. I don't myself know what that means, but it sounds well. Absolute denial that the vote will improve the economic position of women. Indirect influence of women quite sufficient. Emphatic, nay passionate, insistence on your own brainlessness – that is very important. A few passing allusions to us Suffragists as obscure vulgarians. I think you might almost call us uneducated. Yes, uneducated and obscure vulgarians. That also sounds well. And as there's so little to say, it must sound well, my dear girl, or else the Cause perishes. Ah, yes, and you mustn't forget to refer to yourselves as 'so-called traitresses to the sex, so-called survivals of the Dark Ages', because that will elicit respectful sympathy. And be sure and mention that you have joined the Territorial Nursing Corps. I forget its name, but that's near enough. Have you joined it, by the way?

Lady Geraldine (*who is standing all this splendidly*)   No.

Dr Alice   Then do so at once, because that's a piece of subtle cleverness. You disclaim physical force, and yet are preparing indirectly to defend your country. There now, haven't I been a brick? Haven't I wiped out for ever the obligation of those French compositions?

Lady Geraldine (*with spirit but good temper*)   No, that obligation could never be wiped out. And besides, this service doesn't count. Do you know what I'm going to do with this speech? Look.

She throws it into the fire.

Dr Alice   Well, of all the ungrateful, aristocratic little wretches –

Lady Geraldine (*With increased spirit and charm, turning to the others*)   Do you know what I'm going to do next? I'm going home to think.

Dr Alice   Impossible! You've never done such a thing in your life!

Baillie   Shame, Dr Alice! It's never too late to mend – I mean to think!

Lady Geraldine (*smiling at her*)   I should love to come to one of your lectures. May I?

Baillie   Of course you may.

Lady Geraldine (*to* **Gertrude Silberthwaite**)   And will you really paint my portrait?

Silberthwaite   Of course I will. Full face. And when you're thinking!

Lady Geraldine (*to* **Hilda Crowninshield**)   The same language, votes or no votes?

Crowninshield   Yes, yes.

Lady Geraldine (*to* **Nellie Grant**)   Will you let me have your last remaining copy of your paper?

Nellie Grant (*delighted*)   Here it is, Lady Geraldine – a present from us all!

Lady Geraldine   Thank you. Goodbye – all of you. Goodbye!

She goes to the door. When she has reached it, she turns round to **Dr Alice**. *There is a rogueish look on her face.*

Lady Geraldine   Alice. How long do mumps take?

Dr Alice   Oh, about two or three weeks

Lady Geraldine   Very infectious, aren't they?

Dr Alice   Highly.

Lady Geraldine   I believe I've got them already! Afraid I shan't be able to take that Chair! Goodbye!

She goes out. They look after her for a moment.

Dr Alice (*fiercely*)   Mind, if you betray my schoolchum, I'll never speak to you again.

Nellie Grant   Betray one of our own, Dr Alice! For she is one of our own already. Before many weeks have passed she'll be selling Votes for Women in a blinding snowstorm in the merry month of May!

Baillie (*raising her tea cup*)   Her health!

They drink her health.

CURTAIN

Pot and Kettle

Cicely Hamilton and Christopher St John

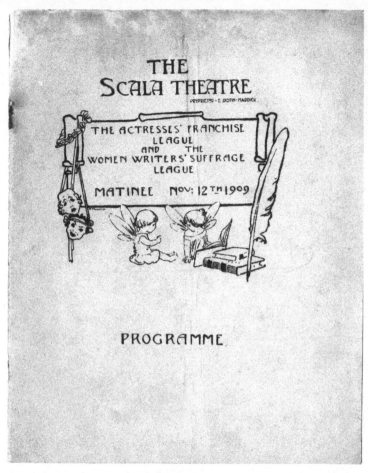

3 Scala Theatre Programme for Actresses' Franchise League
and Women Writers' Suffrage League Matinee, 1909.
Courtesy of Mary Evans Picture Library/The Women's Library.

First performed at the Scala Theatre, London on 12 November 1909.

Mr Brewster – Mr C. Stewart
Mrs Brewster – Miss Marianne Caldwell
Marjorie Brewster – Miss Madge Titheradge
Ernest Hobbs, her fiancé – Mr Ben Field
Nell Roberts, a Suffragette – Miss Elaine Inescourt.
Produced under the direction of Mr E. Harcourt Williams.

Scene: *A Sitting room in a Suburban Villa.*

Mrs Brewster *is sitting by the fire with a small table by her side on which is placed 'the greatest thing that the English have ever done in fiction' – Debrett's Peerage.*

Mr Brewster *is steadily playing Patience at another little table and counting out loud.*

Ernest Hobbs *is fidgetting about the room.*

Ernest　Why did she say she'd be back at 9.30 if she wasn't going to be? It's simply rotten. A chap asked me to go to the Merry Widow – but as Marjorie said she'd be back from her old meeting early, I – oh it's rotten.

Mrs Brewster　Lady Luxton before her marriage was the Honourable Sophia Maze . . . Ah, of course. A daughter of one of the dear Queen's bridesmaids.

Ernest　If I'd gone, it would have been the fiftieth time. I might have got something out of George Edwardes for establishing a record.

Mrs Brewster (*to her husband*)　Do you hear Frederick? Lady Luxton – Baroness Luxton, I should say, is to be on the platform tonight, too. Ernest, dear, can't you settle down to some occupation? Why not play Patience, or take a book?

Mr Brewster　Do you know the Wellington Patience? They may well call it that. It wants the Iron Duke to play it, – 'Knave – Queen'– (*disgustedly*) I don't believe any one has ever done it.

Nell (*putting her head in at the door*)　Where can I find a tray, Aunt Maria? Jane's gone to bed. (*seeing* **Ernest**) Oh, how d'ye do.

Ernest (*stiffly*)　How d'ye do

Mrs Brewster　There ought to be one on the shelf – just outside the kitchen door.

Nell   Thanks

Exit **Nell.**

Ernest   Is Marjorie going to these meetings, often?

Mrs Brewster   She has joined the Anti-Suffrage Society, so I suppose she will have to attend their meetings.

Ernest   I call it rot.

Mrs Brewster   It will put the dear child in the way of meeting some really nice people. Didn't I tell you that it was Lady Shiplake herself who asked Marjorie to buy a ticket?

Ernest (*under his breath*)   Yes, you did, three times

Mrs Brewster   I was so glad I was in when she called with the ticket. Such nice manners – and she seemed to take quite a fancy to Marjorie! She is to be one of the speakers tonight. I'm sure she will make a beautiful speech.

Ernest   Seems to me if it's nobs you want, you can get a stare at them without going to stodgy meetings. I've seen the Queen several times at the Merry Widow.

Mrs Brewster   I trust I have sufficient manners not to *stare* at Lady Shiplake when she calls.

Mr Brewster   Who is this widow to whom you are so constantly referring?

Ernest   I say, Mr Brewster! You aren't going to tell me you've never heard of a play that's been on two years?

Mr Brewster   I take no interest in plays, nor would I go to see one, unless it were by Shakespeare, whose works are sadly neglected.

Ernest   Oh, I don't know about that! They had Hamlet or Pete, or something, at the Lyceum quite lately.

Mrs Brewster   We lead a very quiet life, you know, Ernest. We are old-fashioned, and think there is nothing so pleasant as a quiet evening at home.

Enter **Nell.**

Nell May I have that table?

Mrs Brewster Oh, be careful of my peerage.

Mr Brewster What are you doing, my dear?

Nell Getting Marjorie some supper, Uncle Frederick. Aunt Maria told me she didn't have a thing before she went. I've made her a salad – well, it's the final thing in salads, and as the dining room smells a little of – well of dinner, I thought Marjorie should have her bite in here.

Ernest (*sneeringly*) You're becoming quite domesticated, Miss Roberts.

Nell It's just as well, isn't it, now that Marjorie's political views take her out so much. It's up to someone to come and see that Aunt Maria and Uncle Frederick are getting on all right.

Ernest I'm very glad that Marjorie's on the right side, any how – with ladies, who are really ladies – not with a lot of female roughs who bite policemen, and actually think the word 'obey' ought to be left out of the marriage service!

Nell What a strikingly faithful description of Suffragettes!

Ernest I don't want to describe 'em, but I'd jolly well like to see 'em all whipped. Goodbye Mrs Brewster, I don't think I'll wait any longer.

Mrs Brewster Marjorie will be dreadfully disappointed.

Mr Brewster When I was a young man –

Ernest Perhaps I'll look in again later. A pal of mine's got a studio in London Road. I'll go round and see him to fill in time. You can tell Marjorie I may be coming back. (*Exit.*)

Mrs Brewster He's put out at her being so late – it's only natural.

Nell Quite so, holding the views he does about women interfering in politics, I can quite understand that he feels annoyed at finding his best girl neglecting him for a political meeting. This precious Anti-Suffrage League of yours has quite a lot to answer for.

Mrs Brewster   The Anti-Suffrage League is not a political society.

Nell   Then what the Dickens is it?

Mr Brewster (*pompously – as if quoting*)   A union of right-minded men and women pledged to defend that most sacred of all institutions – the Home.

Nell   What's in a name! That which we call a political meeting by any other name is just as noisy. 'Unions of right-thinking men and women' sounds very nice, and judging from the time she has been there, Marjorie finds it very engrossing.

Mr Brewster   Here she is!

Enter **Marjorie.** *Her veil is down, her manner depressed. Voice, when she speaks, trembling and constrained.*

Nell   Well, old girl, here you are

Mrs Brewster   You're late, darling – we were wondering where you'd got to, and so was Ernest.

Marjorie   Is Ernest here?

Mrs Brewster   No, he couldn't wait, but he may look in again on his way home – to see you're all right after the excitement.

Nell   You look dead fagged. Come along and have some grub.

Mrs Brewster   Nell's got your supper all ready for you.

Marjorie   I don't want any supper!

Mr Brewster   Not want any supper!

Mrs Brewster   Nonsense, dearie –

Nell   Of course it's nonsense – you want it badly. I know what these meetings are. They take it out of you. Come on (*pushes her into chair*) Fall to – cold beef, salad, cheese, stewed fruit.

Mr Brewster   And how did it all go off?

Nell (*helping* **Marjorie** *to food*)   Yes, how did it all go off?
Decorous enthusiasm, eh? Cheers for the wife, cheers for the
mother, cheers for the 'appy, 'appy 'ome? Gentlemen in white
waistcoats assuring you how they reverenced their mothers in
spite of the fact that they considered them far too idiotic to vote.
The county is in danger, chivalry, men are men and women are
women, and all the rest of it – eh?

Marjorie   Don't –

Mr Brewster (*stiffly*)   Perhaps, Nell, you will have the
courtesy to remember that your jeers are out of place in an
old-fashioned household, where we are not in sympathy with
your peculiar ideas on these subjects.

Nell   Righto . . . Did you carry your resolution?

Marjorie   I – I don't know.

Nell   You don't know?

Marjorie   No – that's to say I can't be sure. There was such a
disturbance at the end I couldn't make out.

Nell (*excitedly*)   Good Lord, to think what a treat I've missed. I
could kick myself when I think of it. I'd have given my best hat
to be there – and a pair of boots thrown in.

Mrs Brewster   Really, Nell – you astound me –

Nell   There was a good old opposition then?

Marjorie   There were some Suffragettes – lots of them. The
beasts.

Nell   Steady on, steady on. I shall have to take a leaf out
of Uncle Frederick's book and remind you that I'm not in
sympathy with your peculiar ideas on these subjects.

Marjorie (*almost in tears*)   They *are* beasts.

Nell (*kindly*)   Well, never mind – there's no need to worry
about it if we are. And one beast has made you some quite
decent salad dressing. Try it.

Mrs Brewster   Never mind the Suffragettes, darling – we don't want to hear about *them*. Tell us about dear Lady Shiplake. What did she say?

Nell   Something about woman's true sphere of influence.

Mrs Brewster   I did not ask you, Nell. You were not there, so you can't possibly know.

Nell   It's a safe enough guess, though. They all say it.

Mrs Brewster (*ignoring* **Nell**)   Tell me, darling – what did she say?

Marjorie   I don't know – I can't remember.

Nell   Lady Shiplake is evidently an interesting and impressive speaker.

Mrs Brewster   I must ask you, Nell –

Marjorie (*suddenly bursting into tears*)   Oh, don't – oh, go away.

All   Marjorie – what's the matter?

Marjorie   Oh, I'm so miserable.

Mrs Brewster   Marjorie, darling –

Nell   She's excited – over tired

Marjorie   No, I'm not – it's not that – oh, oh, oh.

Mrs Brewster   What is it, darling – tell me.

Mr Brewster   Something awful.

Mrs Brewster   Marjorie, tell me.

Marjorie   Oh, I can't tell you, I can't. I don't know how I shall ever tell you.

Mrs Brewster   Marjorie – you frighten me. For heaven's sake.

Nell   Here, buck up old girl – drink a drop of water.

Marjorie (*pushing her away*)   Oh, I wish I was dead – I wish I was dead and buried and cremated.

Nell   Pull yourself together, Marjorie. You're frightening Aunt Maria. Now then, out with it – let's know the worst.

Marjorie   *tries to control herself.*

Mrs Brewster   Is it anything about Ernest?

Marjorie (*crying afresh*)   N-no-not yet – but it will be.

Mr Brewster   What do you mean, child?

Marjorie   I don't know what Ernest will say. I don't know what you'll all say. Oh. I'm so miserable – so mi-miserable!

Nell   But why – what has happened.

Marjorie   I'm going – I'm going to – I'm going to be had up –

Mrs Brewster   Had up?

Marjorie   In the police court!

All   What!

Marjorie (*sobs*)

Nell   But – what for? What's the charge?

Marjorie   Assault and b-battery.

All   What!

Nell   Assault and battery – you!

Marjorie   Yes – that's what they said.

Nell   But who did you assault? Who did you batter?

Marjorie   A s-suffragette

Nell   Heavens!

Mrs Brewster   Marjorie, Marjorie, oh, my poor child, what – what have they been doing to you?

Mr Brewster (*agitated*)   Calm yourself, Marjorie. Stop crying, wipe your eyes. For heavens sake, be calm. This must be explained – we must get to the bottom of it. I am to understand – you tell me – that you, my daughter, are to be charged in a common police-court with assaulting and battering one of those unsexed monsters known as suffragettes.

Marjorie   Yes –

Mr Brewster   But it's a lie – it's an infamous lie!

Marjorie   It isn't!

Mrs Brewster   Marjorie!

Mr Brewster (*after a pause*)   It isn't – You tell me that! Child, think what you are saying – think what these words mean. You are out of your senses – grief has distracted you.

Marjorie   No – oh, father, father, I can't think how I came to do it, but I did.

Mr Brewster   You did. (*Drops into a chair and covers his face with his hands.*)

Mrs Brewster   Marjorie! (*Covers her face with her handkerchief.*)

Marjorie   It's no use saying I didn't. Lots of people saw me. The policeman at the door – he saw me. And dozens of suffragettes. And they're all coming as witnesses – to the court – oh, oh, oh!

Mr Brewster (*sepulchrally*)   Maria – it will be in the Mail.

Mrs Brewster   Oh, Frederick! (*Sobs loudly.*)

Nell   I say, Aunt Maria, don't – These things will happen in the best regulated meetings.

Mrs Brewster (*hysterically*)   Go away – It will bring my grey hairs with sorrow to the grave.

Marjorie   Oh, how shall I tell Ernest. He'll never forgive me – never. He said he could never marry anyone but a womanly woman. And now I'm not a womanly woman any more. He'll say I'm as bad as a suffragette. I think I'd better drown myself before I disgrace you all – or take rat poison or prussic acid.

Mrs Brewster   Oh, my child – my one and only child in the felon's dock.

Nell   Shut up, Aunt Maria. Felon's dock – why you might be there for not paying a dog license. Now then, Marjorie, don't go on howling. I dare say something can be done – I'm not so frightened of police courts as you are and I know a lot more about 'em. Now tell me all about it – how did it happen?

Marjorie   There was a – a lady sitting next to me at the meeting –

Nell   Yes?

Marjorie   She had on a fawn coat and a black hat with daisies in it; but she was really a suffragette – though I didn't know it. She looked just like anyone else.

Nell   Some of us do. Go on.

Marjorie   At first she sat quite quiet and I had no idea – I only thought her hat was rather smart. But when dear Lady Shiplake got up and began to read her speech then she put her hand to her mouth – like this – and called out.

Nell   Oh! What did she say?

Marjorie   She said 'Madam, why are you not at home?' in a perfect roar.

Mr Brewster   Disgraceful!

Nell   And that was when you –

Marjorie   No – not then. I was disgusted with her of course, but I was quite dignified. I only said 'You are a very rude and vulgar person.'

Mrs Brewster   Quite right.

Nell   And what did she say?

Marjorie   Nothing. She only laughed.

Nell   Well?

Marjorie   After that, she went on interrupting when Lord Camberwell – he made a lovely speech, I nearly cried – when he said 'Men and men and women are women' she jumped up on her seat and shouted 'Now we are hearing something!' One of the stewards said he'd take her out if she didn't behave – I wish he had. Then she hissed and clapped in all the wrong places, and cheered all the wrong things.

Mr Brewster   Abominable.

Nell   Go on.

Marjorie   Well, at last – at the very end, after all the speeches – the lady in the chair – the chairwoman – got up and said she was going to put the resolution to the meeting. And then there was the most awful row. All the suffragettes – there were hundreds of them – got up and stood on their seats and shouted. They all said they wanted to ask questions; but nobody would let them. So they went on shouting. And she – the one next to me – was about the worst of all. She had got a flag hidden under her coat – with 'Votes for Women' on it – and she took it and waved it. And she kept calling out 'Madam Chairman, I want to put a question to Lady Shiplake.' And at last I got so excited – with all the noise and the organist beginning 'God Save the King' to stop the questions – that I told her to sit down. But she didn't take any notice and went on waving her flag and making more noise. So then I got more excited still – and I don't know exactly what made it do it, but I knocked her hat over her eyes and thumped her twice.

Mr Brewster   You did!

Mrs Brewster   Oh, Marjorie!

Marjorie   I told you lots of people saw me do it – it wasn't any good pretending, . . . The policeman at the door saw me – and she called him –

Mr Brewster   The policeman?

Marjorie   Yes – and – and –

Mr Brewster (*between his teeth*)   Go on – go on to the bitter end.

Marjorie   She said she was going to charge me with assaulting her – that I belonged to the militant section of the anti-suffragettes and she didn't approve of their tactics – and that it would take us down a peg to have the case brought into court – and – oh it was dreadful. I had to give my name and address – and I've got to appear. Don't ask me any more – don't – it was so awful.

Mrs Brewster (*hysterically*)   Oh, what have we done that this blow should fall upon us?

Nell (*under her breath*)   Oh, dry up. Look here, Marjorie, do you know her name – who was she?

Marjorie   That's the worst of it.

Nell   Why – what do you mean?

Marjorie   She's – she's a very important person – very

Nell   Who?

Marjorie (*in a trembling voice*)   Her name is Lady – Lady Susan Pengarvon.

Mrs Brewster   What!

Nell   Lady Susie!

Mr Brewster   Lady Susan Pengarvon, did you say?

Mrs Brewster   Youngest daughter of the late Marquess of Penzance – sister of the present peer.

Marjorie   Yes.

Mr Brewster   And you hit her – a lady of title!

Marjorie   I didn't know –

Mrs Brewster   A Marquess's daughter – and you called her a rude and vulgar person! Oh Marjorie –

Marjorie (*weeping*)   how was I to tell – ?

Nell   Of course not. Marquess's daughters don't go about with labels round their necks, and as it happens, since you had to punch somebody's head I'm jolly glad you punched Lady Susie's.

Mrs Brewster   Nell – you forget yourself

Nell   Can I use your phone, Uncle Frederick? Where is it. Oh there. Buck up Marjorie – never say die. I'll see what I can do for you.

Marjorie   What do you mean?

Nell (*at the telephone*)   3873 Gerrard!

Marjorie   Oh, Father, do you think there is any hope – could she possibly –

Mr Brewster   It is possible she may have some influence – one never knows – these suffragettes are as thick as thieves with one another. It is hardly likely she can ever have met Lady Susan; but she may know someone who knows her – We must hope for the best.

Nell   Now then Exchange – hurry up 3873

Marjorie   Oh, I don't know what I shall do – Think of Ernest –

Nell   Engaged? Get me through as soon as you can.

Marjorie   Do you remember what he said the other day – that a woman who resorted to violence ought to be horsewhipped and then ducked.

Mrs Brewster   Oh, why did we ever listen to Lady Shiplake? Why did we let you join the anti-suffrage society – why didn't we keep you safe at home!

Mr Brewster   You're right, Maria – you're right. It is unfair to blame Marjorie too much. We ought never to have allowed ourselves to be led away. These people are frauds – their position is ridiculous. They tell our innocent child her place is home – and insist on selling her a ticket for a public meeting. They tell our innocent child that she must take no interest in politics – and plunge her into the frenzied atmosphere of a riotous political gathering. The blame is their's, not her's. It was they who lured her away from her domestic duties, they who taught her to neglect the fireside they profess to defend. If they had been practising their own teaching – if they had all been at home darning their stockings, this would not have happened. These women are following in the tracks of the suffragettes! They are spreading the doctrines of the suffragettes, and like the suffragettes, they are wrecking the home they profess to stand for, and they are too stupid to see it.

Nell (*clapping*)   Bravo!

(*Telephone bell rings.*)

Hallo, expect I'm through. (*goes to telephone*)

Mr Brewster   Look at the misery they have already brought upon one peaceful household. The next time I see Lady Shiplake I shall tell her what I think of her and her preposterous goings-on!

Mrs Brewster   Oh, Frederick– you won't.

Mr Brewster   Well, perhaps not, but I should like to.

Nell (*at the telephone*)   Hallo! Are you 3873 Gerrard? That you, Susie?

Marjorie (*astounded*)   Susie! Do you think?

Nell   Yes I know – I have been hearing all about it. You seem to have had a cheerful picnic!– Yes – I have heard that too – What!– Oh!– Put a piece of beefsteak on, that will keep down the swelling! Now shut up and listen to me. You've got to withdraw this charge – What's that – Well *I'll* be hanged if you *don't.* No, I've not gone quite mad – I have not joined the antis. But the girl who gave you your black eye is my cousin and you've got to let her off. I know it's asking a lot, but if you knew how sorry she is I'm sure you would be merciful. You're used to appearing in police courts but she isn't; kindly take that into account – What? – Yes, I know it would have been an awful lark and I'm awfully sorry to disappoint you – but do, Susie, there's a good old soul. Yes, I know – of course she was an idiot – but what else can you expect from an anti? If you drag my respectable family into the police court I'll never speak to you again – What's that? – Good old girl! Eh!– Oh, all right. Tomorrow, at one? Good night. (*hangs up receiver*)

Cheer up Marjorie. Cheer up all of you – no Holloway Castle for you this time. Lady Susan withdraws the charge –

All   Nell!

Marjorie   *flings herself into her arms.*

Nell   That's all right. Even beasts aren't so black as they're painted.

Mr Brewster (*incredulously*)   Then you know – you're acquainted with Lady Susan Pengarvon?

Nell   Rather. She's quite a pal of mine. She and I were chucked out of the Ladies' Gallery the night the grille was shifted.

Marjorie   I don't know how to thank you.

Nell   Rot. Lady Susie's a ripping good sort really – though she does get a bit out of hand when there are antis about – it's all over and done with so don't cry any more – she asked me to apologize and said she hoped I'd bring you to lunch tomorrow so that she might shake hands and show there was no ill-feeling – she'd have come round here but she is such a sight with her black eye.

Marjorie   Oh –

Mrs Brewster   To lunch – Lady Susan Pengarvon has asked Marjorie to lunch. Frederick, do you hear?

Enter **Ernest.**

Ernest   Hallo, Marjorie – you are back then – at last.

Marjorie (*nervously*)   Yes, I'm back –

Ernest   Why, what's the matter with you? How white you look – anything up –

Marjorie   Oh no – only –

Nell (*quickly*)   Can't you see she's dead beat. You shouldn't let her go to these meetings. She's not used to them and they're too much for her – the heat and the noise –

Ernest   Did any of those blessed suffragettes get in?

Nell   Yes – that's it. However, she met a friend of mine there – a very jolly woman – Lady Susan Pengarvon – who has asked her to lunch tomorrow.

Ernest   What ho!

Mrs Brewster   A sister of the present Marquess of Penzance.

Ernest   What ho! We are getting on. This is what comes of joining the Anti-Suffrage League, eh?

Nell   Just so. All the same I should make her chuck the Anti-Suffrage League, if I were you. It's too strenuous altogether. If she must belong to something let her pick out something quieter – the Women's Freedom League, or the WSPU. . .

As she goes out the CURTAIN FALLS.

Miss Appleyard's Awakening

Evelyn Glover

4 Adeline Bourne (1862–1965), one of the founding
members of the Actresses' Franchise League.
Photograph by Dover Street Studios, 1912.

Evelyn Glover 1874–1941

Evelyn Glover was born in Lancashire in 1874 and had a long and successful career as a writer. Her plays include *A Question of Time* (1908) – co-written with F. Mathias Alexander, *A Chat with Mrs. Chicky* (1912), *Showin' Samyel* (1914), *A Bit of Blighty* (1916), *Their Mothers* (1917), *Time to Wake Up* (1919) and *Thieves in the Night* (1921). Glover wrote several short pieces for BBC Radio that were broadcast between 1927 and 1934 and a children's series for BBC Radio, *The Careful Queen* (1934–35). In her final publication, a memoir called *Cats and My Camera* (London: M. Joseph, 1938), she describes fellow suffrage playwright Beatrice Harraden as a 'dear friend'.

Characters

Miss Appleyard
Mrs Crabtree (her visitor)
Morton (her Parlourmaid)

Miss Appleyard's Awakening was first performed at the Rehearsal Theatre, London, on 20 June 1911.

It was published by the AFL in 1911.

Scene: *A Drawing-room.*

Time: *During an Election.*

Morton *is discovered arranging blinds, tidying up the room etc. Enter* **Miss Appleyard** *in outdoor things.*

Miss A Oh Morton, I must have some tea now – I really can't wait till half past four. I don't think there's anything in the world so tiring as canvassing!

Morton I hope you got a proper lunch, 'm?

Miss A No, it wasn't at all proper – two stale sandwiches at Owen's – but I couldn't get home. The dinner hour was the best time for catching some of the men. Fancy, Morton, I've got three fresh promises for Mr Sharp!

Morton How splendid, 'm! Were you up by the factory?

Miss A Yes, in Dale Street and Quebec Street. I begin to think half the idiots in Mudford must have settled there judging from the intelligence of some of the voters I've been arguing with this morning!

Morton Won't you go and lie down a bit, 'm? You look tired out.

Miss A Oh no, I shall be all right when I've had some tea. I should have been home earlier only I simply couldn't get through the crowd in Nevil Square where one of those dreadful Suffragists was speaking. I really could shake the lot of them!

Morton I suppose she was talking about votes for women, 'm?

Miss A Oh yes, I suppose so – I didn't really listen. I heard something about some bill they wanted to get passed. The less women have to do with bills the better, to my mind – Parliamentary *and* other kinds.

Morton I daresay she'd plenty to say, 'm?

Miss A   I daresay she had, Morton. I wish I'd been near enough to tell her to go back and look after her home and leave Parliament to manage its own affairs! Oh by the way, Morton, if you and Cook would like to go to Mr Sharp's meeting at the Town Hall tonight I think the house might be shut up for a couple of hours. I can take my key in case I get back first.

Morton   Thank you, 'm, we should very much.

Miss A   Well tell Cook, then. You could manage to get off my half past seven, couldn't you, as I'm having dinner earlier? She'll have no washing up to speak of.

Morton   Oh yes, 'm.

Miss A   Don't leave it later because the place is going to be crowded. (*Looks at her hands.*) I'm too dirty to eat – those factory chimneys were simply raining blacks! I'll be ready in 2 minutes. (*Exits.*)

Exit **Morton** *and returns with tea cloth, putting it on table and humming 'March of the Women'. While she is doing this a bell rings outside. She ignores it, and it rings again.*

Morton   All right – all right! Somebody else has got things to do as well as you!

Exit, to reappear almost immediately and usher in a visitor.

Morton   What name shall I say, please?

Mrs C   Miss Appleyard wouldn't know my name. Just say that a lady from the Anti-Suffrage Society would be much obliged if she could speak to her.

Morton   Thank you, 'm.

Mrs C   I won't keep her more than a moment or two. Oh – er – I shall be asking her to allow you and your fellow servants to sign a petition I've got with me. How many of you are there?

Morton   Two, 'm.

Mrs C   Not more? Still, two names are something.

Morton   What is the petition about, 'm?

Mrs C   About? – Oh it would take rather long to explain. But *you* don't want women to sit in Parliament and leave their homes to go to rack and ruin, do you?

Morton: Oh no, 'm.

Mrs C   And you don't want every woman in England to have a vote so that they can swamp the men and govern the country themselves?

Morton   That's never what the Suffragists want, is it 'm?

Mrs C   Oh they'll all *tell* you they don't, but of course they do really. When a woman leaves her own duties to take up a man's she soon loses her sense of truth and everything else.

Morton   Really, 'm?

Mrs C   Why this very petition you were asking about it against a set of women who pretend that they don't think their sex ought to meddle with politics and yet they're working themselves in this Election as hard as they can!

Morton   Oh that doesn't seem right, 'm, does it?

Mrs C   Right? It's very wicked and deceitful, of course but that's just an example of the sort of thing that happens when a woman interferes with –

She stops short as **Miss Appleyard** *enters the room and looks round inquiringly.*

Morton   A lady to see you, 'm. (*Exit.*)

Mrs C   Good afternoon, Miss Appleyard, hope I'm not disturbing you? I'm afraid you're just going out?

Miss A   No, I've just come in. Please sit down.

Mrs C   I won't detain you more than a few minutes. My name is Crabtree – Mrs Crabtree. I've come as a delegate from the Mudford ASS – I understand that you belong to it?

Miss A   The ASS?

Mrs C   The Anti-Suffrage Society.

Miss A   Oh, I beg your pardon. I didn't recognize those rather unfortunate initials for the moment. Yes, I've been a member for nearly a year, I think. A friend of mine gave me no peace till I said she might send in my name.

Mrs C   We have one or two noble proselytizers! They stop at nothing!

Miss A   Oh, I'd no real objection – I've always steadily declined to listen to anything on the subject of Women's Suffrage.

Mrs C   I wish there were more like you! I've really come to ask if you would be good enough to sign a petition that some of us are getting up?

Miss A   Certainly. I never refuse my name to any Anti-Suffrage Petition. I should think I've signed four this month.

Mrs C   How splendid of you! And yet Suffragists say we don't work for our cause!

Miss A   But Suffragists will say anything! I suppose you've read the accounts of the disgraceful disturbances in Liverpool last night?

Mrs C   No. Were there any? I can't say that I trouble my head much about that sort of thing.

Miss A   But don't you think it's abominable?

Mrs C   There are worse things in connection with the Suffrage movement than disturbances.

Miss A   Worse?

Mrs C   Very much worse.

Miss A   But what *could* be worse?

Mrs C   Oh my dear Miss Appleyard, if a woman's in a policeman's arms – of course it's very deplorable, but at least you know where she *is*!

Miss A Certainly – but –

Mrs C And if she's shouting in the market place like the female I saw addressing crowds in Nevil Square just now – at all events she's fighting you in the open!

Miss A Of course.

Mrs C Even if she's never done anything for her side but join a Suffrage Society – well, you do know she's against you.

Miss A Certainly, but I'm afraid I don't quite see what you mean to imply.

Mrs C What should you say to *traitors within the camp*?

Miss A Traitors within the camp?

Mrs C Traitors within the camp, Miss Appleyard. Women who join *Anti*-Suffrage Societies and under the cloak of membership go about propagating the very ideas they pretend to abhor!

Miss A You can't possibly be serious!

Mrs C I thought I should startle you. My firm belief is that they're in the pay of the Suffragists.

Miss A But how perfectly disgraceful! I hadn't the slightest idea that such a thing existed! Surely it can be stopped?

Mrs C We hope so – we believe so. That is the object of the petition I'm asking you to sign. (*Draws paper from long envelope.*) We want some pronouncement from headquarters in London that will make treachery of this kind impossible.

Miss A That's an excellent idea. I'll sign it with pleasure.

Mrs C Thank you very much. And I hope you'll allow your servants to do the same?

Miss A My servants?

Mrs C Well it swells a list of signatures so beautifully – especially if a large staff is kept. Lady Carter's signed to the boot boy!

Miss A   I'm afraid I don't keep a boot-boy and I have only two servants. I've never really asked them their views on the Suffrage.

Mrs C   Their views? I didn't ask my servants their views. I merely sent the petition to the kitchen for signatures. Nobody will think we're in earnest if we don't get plenty.

Miss A   Well to be quite frank with you, one rather hesitates – I mean it might be little difficult for a servant to refuse her mistress, mightn't it?

Mrs C   Refuse! Oh, of course I don't press the point for a moment, Miss Appleyard. We shall be only too pleased if you will give us your own signature.

Miss A   May I have the petition? I always write particularly badly when I inscribe my name on a public document. Do you want full Christian names? I've got four.

Mrs C   They would look imposing.

Miss A   As you say, treachery within the camp must be put down at any cost. One can hardly believe that women would stoop to it!

Mrs C   I'm surprised at nothing in connection with the Suffrage.

Miss A   I wonder if you're right in thinking that the Suffragists are responsible?

Mrs C   I'm convinced of it

Miss A   Of course the quickest way to stop anything so flagrant would be to show it up in the papers. If you'll give me a few particulars I don't in the least mind writing a letter to the *Spectator.*

Mrs C   Oh that would be splendid! There's every excuse for a woman to come out into the open in an exceptional case like this. Besides you could use a *nom de plume*

Miss A   I haven't the slightest objection to signing my name to any letter I write.

Mrs C Just as you like, of course. A name often does work wonders. I've got twenty three to my petition already.

Miss A I'd better complete your second dozen before we discuss the matter further. After all, though one must make a stand against it, conduct of this sort is bound to defeat its own ends. Every decent-minded woman will turn from it in disgust.

Mrs C How many decent-minded women will there be left in England if this Suffrage movement goes on?

Miss A Oh come, Mrs Crabtree, we're not all going to bow the knee to Baal! I can't think that the Suffrage has made any open headway in Mudford and you must get this petition sent in time to prevent any secret proselytizing.

Mrs C Prevent? I wish we were in time for that!

Miss A You surely can't mean that there are any of these atrocious women among *us*?

Mrs C I do, Miss Appleyard. I have only too good reason to believe that we are warming a viper in our bosoms!

Miss A Tell me her name! Don't hesitate to mention a name in a case like this!

Mrs C I don't know it yet unfortunately. I'm waiting to discover it before I denounce her openly.

Miss A Nothing would give me greater pleasure than to help you!

Mrs C I wonder if you could! Do you know anything of the streets behind the factory?

Miss A What – Dale Street and Quebec Street do you mean?

Mrs C Yes – with the little red houses where so many of the hands live

Miss A You don't mean to say she's dared to go there?

Mrs Crabtree *looks round, draws a little closer, and lowers her voice.*

Mrs C   Miss Appleyard, I've just been told on excellent authority that a member of our own Anti-Suffrage Society was seen canvassing in Quebec Street and Dale Street this very morning!

There is a moment of absolute silence.

Miss A   C-canvassing?

Mrs C   My dear, you evidently haven't grasped the brazen tactics of these women. They pretend of be Anti-Suffragists and they *canvass*!

Miss A   But surely I – they –

Mrs C   They subscribe – openly – to the tenet that woman is incapable of forming a political opinion, and they not only form one for themselves, but they go about trying to influence those of men!

Miss A   Yes, but you surely –

Mrs C (*working herself up and ignoring any interruption*)   They assert – with us – that woman's place is the home and spend long hours away from their own in the arena of politics!

Miss A   But do you seriously mean that an Anti-Suff –

Mrs C   They profess to leave imperial matters to men with one hand and force their way into meetings at which such matters are discussed with the other!

Miss A   But is it possible that –

Mrs C   They proclaim that political activity tends to break up the harmony of the home and go straight out and address envelopes in Committee rooms by the hour. The insidiousness of it! Of course the ignorant women to whom they talk are drawn into politics in spite of themselves and the way is paved for the Suffragist who works openly! It's a far more dangerous crusade than the militant one, in my opinion, because it wears the guise of an angel of light!

Miss A   I see what you mean, of course. But perhaps it hasn't occurred to them that they're doing – doing all you say!

Mrs C Don't tell me!

Miss A Don't you think they might have never looked at it in that light?

Mrs C Oh my dear Miss Appleyard, one either is or isn't in favour of a thing. You can't do it in practice and denounce it in print, you know!

Miss A I – I never thought of that. Of course it *is* inconsistent.

Mrs C It's worse than inconsistent, to my mind. Personally I strongly disapprove of the way in which I'm sorry to say some of even the leaders of our party try to defend the municipal vote[1] for women. I prefer to be honest and deplore the mistake that granted it to them.

Miss A You don't think women should have the municipal vote?

Mrs C Of course I don't! What is it but a smaller edition of the Parliamentary one? There's merely a difference of degree. The qualities that unfit a woman for one naturally unfit her for the other.

Miss A What qualities do you mean, exactly?

Mrs C Why, Lord Cromer has told us. Hasty generalization – vague and undisciplined sympathies – extreme sentimentality – I can't remember all he said, but it was in the papers. He said they were characteristic of a majority of the female sex.

Miss A Oh, did he?

Mrs C Yes – at a meeting for men only, in Manchester.

Miss A Perhaps it's as well that women weren't admitted.

Mrs C Well, I believe there were a few women on the platform, but I agree with you. I'm not at all in favour of women attending public meetings as a rule, though I *have* made an exception myself to hear Lord Cromer.

Miss A Really?

Mrs C   He's such a marvellous grasp of this subject. There's Lord Curzon, too – of course you know his fifteen reasons against Women's Suffrage?

Miss A   No, I'm afraid I don't.

Mrs C   Oh, I must send them to you! I'm always meaning to learn them by heart. I know the first – 'Political activity will tend to take away woman from her proper sphere and highest duty, which is maternity.'

Miss A   But we can't *all* be mothers.

Mrs C   Oh, he recognizes that! Only no doubt he considers married women particularly because, as he says in a later reason, they, if any, are best qualified to exercise the vote.

Miss A   But I thought he said it would interfere with maternity?

Mrs C   So he did.

Miss A   Then how can he say that married women are best qualified to exercise it?

Mrs C   I don't altogether follow that myself, I admit. I'm content to leave it to a superior brain to my own.

Miss A   And even in the case of mothers – supposing they *had* votes – would they be constantly engaged in political activity? Fathers aren't!

Mrs C   Men are political by nature – women are not. If women got the vote they would have so much to learn that they'd never have time for anything else. (*Goes on as* **Miss Appleyard** *is evidently about to demur but thinks better of it.*) But you must read the reasons yourself – that is if you think it advisable to go into the subject. They set forward so plainly the awful dangers of adding unbalanced judgements to a logical male electorate.

Miss A   I happened to be talking to one of the logical male electorate this morning. He's my chimney sweep. He informed me that he was going to vote for Mr Holland because his own wife is a Dutchwoman.

Mrs C   Really? Which is Mr Holland?

Miss A   Do you mean to say you didn't know that he was the Labour Candidate?

Mrs C   Oh, I must have seen the placards and heard people talking, of course. But I naturally don't take any interest in politics. I don't consider them to be a woman's concern.

Miss A   What *do* you consider to be a woman's concern?

Mrs C   Her HOME!

Miss A   But – do excuse me – you're putting things in rather a new light to me. Don't vague sympathies and sentimentality and – what else did Lord Cromer say? – hasty generalization? – matter in the home?

Mrs C   Oh-er-well – of course it would be better *without* them, but as he says, most women *are* like that. I mustn't trespass longer on your time, Miss Appleyard. If I may have your signature I won't detain you any more.

Miss A   I haven't really looked at the text of this – I'd only surmised it from what you told me. (*Scans paper in silence, then looks up.*) I see it's a request to headquarters that some rule may be framed which shall debar any member of an Anti-Suffrage Society from canvassing.

Mrs C   We thought it better to confine ourselves to the canvassing to start with. Later we hope to attack more of these abominable tactics.

A bell is heard outside.

Miss A (*folding up paper deliberately and handing it back*)   Well, Mrs Crabtree, I may well tell you quite frankly that you wont attack them through me.

Mrs C   Miss Appleyard – I don't understand you!

Miss A   I can't sign that paper.

Mrs C   May I ask why not?

There is a tap at the door.

Miss A   Come in!

Enter **Morton.**

Morton   Excuse me disturbing you a moment, please, 'm.

Miss A   What is it Morton? (*to* **Mrs Crabtree**) Excuse me,
Mrs Crabtree!

Morton   Miss Allbut's called, 'm, and she won't come in, but
she says could you kindly send word if it's ten or half past that
she's to go canvassing with you tomorrow.

Miss A (*firmly*)   Say ten o'clock, please.

Morton   Yes, 'm.

Exit **Morton.**

Miss A   I beg your pardon, Mrs Crabtree. You were asking –

Mrs C   I am answered, Miss Appleyard – I am answered!
Little did I think when I denounced the women among us who
are secretly undermining our influence that they had so far
worked upon your feelings as to persuade you to join them!

Miss A   I really don't understand you. Nobody has worked on
my feelings. I offered to help canvassing this time just as I did at
the last Election. I was going to tell you so when my maid came
in.

Mrs C   Then – then is it possible that you are the woman who
was canvassing in Dale Street and Quebec Street this morning.

Miss A   It's more than possible – it's a fact.

Mrs C   This – this is beyond everything! You consider
yourself capable of forming a political opinion?

Miss A   Well – shall we say at least as capable as the
gentleman whose going to vote for Mr Holland because his own
wife's a Dutchwoman!

Mrs C   You don't think that a woman's place is the home?

Miss A   Place – certainly. Prison – no. You might as well say
that a man's place is his office and blame him for coming home

in an evening or taking an interest in his wife's duties or his children's lessons!

Mrs C (*solemnly and loudly*)   Man is Man and Woman is Woman!

Miss A   Oh I'm quite prepared to concede that.

Mrs C   And conceding it, you actually think that a woman ought to meddle with politics?

Miss A   Meddle? How can any intelligent woman help taking an interest in the affairs of her country?

Mrs C   *Her* country? It's the country of the men who fight for it!

Miss A   You mean that only soldiers and sailors should be politicians?

Mrs C   This is ridiculous! It is only too easy to see what influences have been at work!

Miss A   Would you kindly explain what you mean?

Mrs C   I mean that your line of reasoning is taken straight from the publications of the Suffrage Societies!

Miss A   The publications of the Suffrage Societies? I've never even seen any!

Mrs C   I cannot, of course, dispute your word. But Suffragists think that a woman should take what they call an intelligent interest in the affairs of her country! Suffragists maintain that a woman doesn't unsex herself by political activity. Suffragists declare that the average woman is as capable of forming an opinion in these matters as hundreds of the men voters of today!

Miss A   And so do I!

Mrs C   Then, Miss Appleyard, all I can ask is, what are you doing among *us*?

There is a silence. **Mrs Crabtree** *prepares to leave and continues speaking.*

Mrs C   I am glad that you see that absurdity of your position for yourself. It would be a waste of time to argue further with you today, but I shall never rest until you are back within the true fold. I want every woman to be a perfect woman!

Miss A   It seems to me that you want every woman to be a perfect fool!

Mrs C   Good afternoon, Miss Appleyard.

Miss A   Good afternoon, Mrs Crabtree!

Exit **Mrs Crabtree.**

Miss A (*calls*)   Morton!

Morton   I'm just bringing your tea 'm. (**Morton** *enters with tea things on a tray, and puts them on table.*)

Miss A   Morton, some papers came by post this morning – printed papers from a Suffrage Society. I put them in the waste-paper basket. I supposed they'll have been thrown away by now?

Morton   No, 'm, they've not. Cook and me have got them in the kitchen.

Miss A   I'd rather like to have a look at them.

Morton   I'll bring them, 'm. If you'll excuse my saying so, Cook and me think there's a deal of sound common sense in this Suffrage business.

Miss A   D'you know, Morton, I'm beginning to think it's quite possible that you may be right!

CURTAIN

Note

1   Municipal elections are local town and council elections.

Her Vote

H. V. Esmond

5 Actresses' Franchise League member Eva Moore and actor and playwright H. V. Esmond. Photograph by Bain News Service, c. 1910–15. Courtesy of the Library of Congress, Prints and Photographs Division.

H. V. Esmond 1869–1922

The son of a doctor, H. V. Esmond was born at Hampton
Court and educated privately. He went on the stage in 1885
and married actress and AFL member Eva Moore in 1891. A
hugely successful actor, he also wrote over 25 plays, many of
which were produced in both the West End and on Broadway
including *One Summer's Day* (1897), *The Wilderness* and *When We
Were Twenty-One* (both 1901), *My Lady Virtue* (1902), *Eliza Comes
to Stay* (1913), *Birds of a Feather* (1920) and *Two Jacks and a Jill*
(1921).

First performed at Terry's Theatre, London, on 13 May 1909
with the following cast:

The Girl   Miss Eva Moore
The Drudge   Miss Suzanne Sheldon
The Clerk   Mr H.V. Esmond

First published by Samuel French in 1910.

Scene: *Her father's office. A busy looking room. Large writing table at right of which sits the old* **Clerk** *at work. There is a telephone on the table.*

After a moment's pause the door is flung open and the **Girl** *rustles in full of intention and determination all over her.*

The **Clerk** *looks up from his labours and sighs resignedly on seeing her. She sits down opposite him.*

Girl (*sweetly*)   Good afternoon, Mr Furdew. I hope I don't disturb you.

The **Clerk** *moves important papers from under her parasol and gold purses, etc., that she lavishly disposes on the table.*

Clerk   Not at all, Miss Elizabeth. I'm afraid the lace of your parasol has –

Girl (*moving her parasol*)   Tch! I didn't see the inkpot was open. Is my father in?

Clerk   No, Miss Elizabeth.

Girl   Then I want the telephone.

Clerk   Your father could get no telephone message now, Miss Elizabeth – he's on his way to Leeds.

Girl   I am not telephoning to my father.

Clerk (*apologizing*)   I beg your pardon.

She takes the telephone, and speaks.

Girl   I want 132 Central – please.
   (*a pause*)
   Number engaged – not at all. How annoying they are, it's only because girls are at the other end. If it were a man! Oh, yes; 123 Central? No, no. 132 Central. Which is it? Oh I don't know now – you've put me off with your talking – wait a minute – I'll get the book.(*to* **Clerk**) It's absurd how they hustle one.

Clerk   Quite, Miss.

He hands her the telephone book.

Girl   Thank you so much.

(*She runs through the pages hurriedly.*)

W. W. W. which end of the book is W?

(*The telephone rings – she drops book and seizes it.*)

Yes, what? – Oh, good.

(*She laughs and listens.*)

How are you? – don't be silly, Reggie. I'm in a serious mood.

You were just writing to me were you, how funny, great news have you?

So have I. I've got two seats for the meeting tonight – what meeting?

The meeting the suffragettes!!

What did you say? Rates – no nothing about rates, only indirectly. You said *rats* did you? Well if you say things like that again you'll make me angry – yes, angry! You don't realize that it's a movement.

(*She gives an enormous importance to the word.*)

Yes, a movement. A great movement! and it's of Vital Importance to our Sex. Yes, I said sex. what? You think we're losing sight of it – what the movement? No, the sex! Well I don't mean to lose sight of the movement anyway – it's most vital to us – (*she stamps*) – it doesn't so much matter about the sex – we've all *got* that – we haven't got the other. But it's coming – and what I want to say is I've got these tickets and you must take me to the meeting to-night. What? You're sending me a note? Tell me now. Can't talk it through the 'phone? How funny you men are.

(*She puts 'phone down for a minute and turns sweetly to* **Clerk.**)

I   hope I'm not disturbing you, Mr Honeydew.

Clerk (*grimly*)   Not in the least, Miss Elizabeth.

She grips the 'phone again.

Girl   No, Reggie, I didn't leave the wire – your news is more serious than votes. Reggie, don't be silly – how could it be. Oh, yes – we'll get them – and *you know* we ought to have them because you told me so only last Thursday in Lady Candriff's conservatory. No, it wasn't because the waltz music made you dreamy.

No! I won't be chained to a seat – and what? No! I won't write my views in anybody's blood.

(*Then vehemently stamping.*)

No, No, No – what I say is – there are a million more of us than there are of you, and we are not going to be left in the cold. No, I never said a vote would warm me – but what I say and what all we women say is – something has got to be done. You can't come round for the moment! No, I don't want you – I've joined the movement.

The door is opened cautiously and the **Drudge** *looks in. The* **Clerk** *snaps at her.*

Clerk   Well?

The **Drudge** *rubs her nose with her apron and nods towards the* **Girl**, *who turns sweetly to the* **Clerk.**

Girl   It's all right, Mr Dewdrop. I told her to follow me up – she is in 'the movement.' (*Then to the* **Drudge**, *most graciously.*) Won't you sit on that very hard sofa? (*The* **Drudge** *accepts the invitation.*)

(*The telephone rings again.*)

No, no, I didn't leave the wire, but a lady dropped in who entirely feels with *me* and I merely spoke to her for a moment.

The **Drudge** *is heard to murmer huskily.*

Drudge   I sweeps out these buildin's – I works 'ard, I want a vote.

Girl (*soothingly*)   It's all right – it's coming . . . and oh! then won't it be splendid!!

Drudge (*sadly*)   I 'ankers for it.

Girl   It *will* make *such* a difference to us all. Oh, you've no idea! I, oh, our *status* will be so much improved.

Drudge   My status 'as been a-weighing on me for weeks past.

Girl   So it has on all our sex.

Drudge   I took carbodinate of soda for mine (*very depressed*) – it didn't move it.

Girl (*a little agitated*)   No, no! Our status isn't inside us – it's – as it were – outside – apart, as it were – politics and personal dignity – er – sex prerogatives – I mean prerogatives – (*She makes up her mind not to wrestle with the word and continues as if no accident had happened. Talking to the* **Drudge.**)   Oh, you must go to some of the meetings – it's no good their saying, 'Men are men, and women are women' because we know better than that, don't we? We want to be up and doing, don't we?

Drudge   I'm allus up an' doin'.

Girl   Yes, but I mean in a noble way – not – not practical things but – noble things – things one can't explain even to oneself – you know what I mean.

Drudge (*sadly smoothing her apron – with a far away look in her eyes*)   Yus, it's the vote.

Girl   Oh, I never thought I should feel so enthusiastic about anything as I feel about this – to – to – expand one's mind – to – to open one's arms and grasp the intangible, as it were – it gives us women new life. (*She turns vehemently to the* **Drudge.**) Look at the area. (*Puts back 'phone.*)

The **Drudge** *comes back to facts a little hurt.*

Drudge   Eh!

Girl (*apologetically*)   I don't mean the area you mean – I'm *so* sorry – I mean the – oh, the – well you know what I mean, I think its fine!

Drudge   The last area I scrubbed –

Girl   *Not* that area, I told you. (*Then a little reproachfully.*) I'm afraid you're not being very intelligent – the Political Area – where we shall rule.

Clerk   Will you vote Tariff Reform, Miss Elizabeth?

Girl   Of course – it's a fine thing.

Clerk   You know all the facts?

Girl (*inclined to be truthful – hesitates a little*)   Er – I don't think I know quite *all*.

Clerk   I see – you are content to follow a male leader.

Girl   There's nothing else to follow. (*The **Clerk** returns peacefully to his labours. The **Girl** regards him for a moment with suspicion – again the telephone rings – seizing it.*) That you Reggie? Yes. Oh, yes. My lady friend is still here – what? (*A pause while she listens.*) What an extraordinary request – read her your note out loud – well I never. But – right – I *do* promise to. No, it isn't here yet – then you can't come round yourself. No – Oh, Reggie, yes I *swear* I'll read it out loud and then telephone you straight – right – right – but Reggie, dear old man, it's no use your talking, we want the vote, and what we *want* we *get*. Reggie, I didn't mean to call you 'dear old man' – it slipped out because the telephone was between us. (*She suddenly ripples.*) Oh, Reggie, shut up. (*Then in a hoarse whisper.*) Don't keep talking about her as 'my lady friend', she isn't a friend really, she – she's only an acquaintance. I met her on the office stairs – she is interested in the movement, that's all – you can't hear? Well, I can't shout – she's sitting quite close. (*She turns sweetly to the **Drudge** who shows symptoms of dozing.*) You *are* interested in the movement, aren't you?

Drudge   Yus.

Girl   I knew you were. (*She returns to the telephone.*) What? I'll ask her. Mr Wellington wants to know if you are married –

Drudge   Not up to now.

Girl   And how many children you've got – but of course – hm! passing on to next cage (*she rings off violently and crosses to the* **Drudge**). Mr Wellington has sent me a letter which he says I am to read to you.

Drudge   Life's so lonely – can't 'e give me a vote? I sort of feel I could 'ug it.

Girl (*getting really quite disappointed in her*)   I don't think you quite realize what the vote means to a woman.

Clerk (*looking up*)   What does it, Miss Elizabeth?

Girl   It means so much that I couldn't possibly explain it.

The **Clerk** *sighs and again resumes his labours. The office bell rings, and he rises and goes out.*

Girl (*muses*)   What can he mean by sending me this note. I'll – (*She goes to telephone, irresolute.*) No, I won't – yes, I will. (*And she rings*) 132 Central. (*She gets it.*) Yes, yes, Reggie? Oh, I beg your pardon, Mr Farrow, is that you? – Oh yes, my father is quite well, thank you. I thought I was talking to Mr Wellington. Yes, father says you were quite right about the drains – 'yielding the line to a younger man' – not at all, I merely wanted to – (*shortly*) Oh, that you Reggie? No, I'm not fussing. (*The* **Clerk** *comes in with note.*) Oh, your note's just come – I – (*a long pause*) Cut off. (*She puts down the telephone in disgust and takes note from the* **Clerk** *then turns sweetly to the* **Drudge***.*) Don't you hate the telephone? He's at one end and I'm at the other, it's – ugh!!!

Drudge   I never 'ad a 'e.

Girl   I've got to read this aloud to you – you don't mind, I promised.

(*The* **Drudge** *wearily acquiesces, and the* **Girl** *opens the note and begins.*) 'Elizabeth', that's me. No 'dear' or anything, just 'Elizabeth', shortly, how odd. 'Tell your lady friend to get hold of a good fellow and marry him.'

Drudge (*brightens considerably*)   'Ear, 'ear!

Girl   'Tell her to go home and have a fine large family and bring 'em up to be defenders of the Empire.'

Drudge   'E talks sense – I'm with 'im.

Girl   'As for you, Elizabeth' – (*She turns and beams on the* **Drudge.**) He's talking about *me* now –

Drudge   'E do chat, don't 'e?

Girl   'I have been made junior partner this morning, so we can be married in a fortnight.' (*She squeals a little squeal, then controls herself and resumes reading, hurriedly.*) 'I can't take you to the meeting to-night, I'm too busy, but I *could* spend the entire evening with you if you are likely to be at home – we can be married Thursday week. Telephone reply. Reginald Wellington.' (*She flies to the telephone.*) 132 Central, please. Hullo! Hullo! who's that? – I want Mr Wellington. – He's *out*? No, no! Who are you? – 'His clerk.' 'He's gone to the bar for a sandwich.' I thought they went there for a brief – follow him – find him out wherever he is – tell him I shall be at home – at *home*–my gracious me (*loudly*) I shall be *at home* the *entire* evening. Who am I? Oh, what a fool the man is – all clerks are – I beg your pardon, Mr Faldew.

Clerk   Don't mention it, Miss Elizabeth.

She wheels back to the telephone.

Girl   I – I, Miss Nanson shall be at home the *entire* evening – tell him at once I shall be at home *all* the evening – got that – good! (*She replaces the telephone and sinks into chair exhausted.*) Oh dear, the telephone makes me get hot all over. (*There is a pause – after which she turns sweetly to the* **Clerk.**) I hope I haven't interrupted you, Mr Mildew.

Clerk   Not at all.

Girl   But father doesn't mind my using it when he isn't here and it is useful, isn't it? – Thursday week, isn't it wonderful? (*She wakes out of her dream and rustles around.*) Where *did* I put my gold purse. (*And she proceeds to ransack the table.*)

Drudge (*to herself*)   Go 'ome, 'ave a large family and defend the Empire.

Clerk (*grimly*)   Better finish the office stairs first, Baker!

Drudge (*rising*)   Yus, sir! (*And she wakes out of her dream.*)

Girl (*has collected her belongings*)   Here's my purse – (*She turns rippling with inward joy, and sees the* **Drudge.**) Oh, I'm so sorry – I forgot you for the moment – but I hadn't forgotten you really – I'm so glad we've had this talk. Oh! And (*with great graciousness*) you can have my ticket for the meeting to-night – I'm afraid I shall be too busy to use it now – but *you'll* use it *won't you?* You won't *back out* – it's so cowardly to back out – if you women don't stick together, your cause will never advance – you must show a bold front or nothing will be accomplished.

Drudge   Ain't *you* goin' to the meetin'?

Girl   Oh no! Not now – I – er – circumstances have arisen – I'd sooner you had my ticket – I'm going to have a little chat with Reggie. (*And she ripples out of the office.*)

Clerk (*grimly*)   Let's get back to our work.

Drudge (*looking dreamily at the meeting ticket*)   Yus, sir.

CURTAIN

The Mother's Meeting

Mrs Harlow Phibbs

6 Members of the Actresses' Franchise League on a Suffrage march.
Photograph by Barrett's Photo Press.

Mrs Harlow Phibbs 1864–1932

Mrs Harlow Phibbs (nee Frances Clarke) was the wife of
Church of England Curate in Hastings and appears to have
been very active in the Suffrage movement there, attending
local Suffrage meetings, Suffrage demonstrations in London
and leading the local Women's Suffrage Choir. She wrote *The
Rack* (1912) and is very probably the author of *Jim's Leg* (1911),
another suffrage comic monologue featuring a working class
character. It is attributed to an 'L. S. Phibbs' – Frances Phibbs'
two middle names were Lena and Stanley, and so therefore it is
likely that she was L. S. Phibbs.

The Mother's Meeting was published in 1913 by the AFL.

Enter **Mrs Puckle** *in purple or green hat, trimmed with purple and green feathers.*[1] *She wears a black coat or cape, and a clean apron, and carries a bundle of work. There is on the stage a little table and a chair.* **Mrs Puckle**, *as if greeting friends, stands before them with complacent air.*

Mrs Puckle   Bit surprised to see me, eh?

(*She advances, puts her work on table.*)

You'll be more surprised when you hear where I've been.

(*She sinks as if exhausted into chair, and wipes her face with a large, clean handkerchief which she shakes out of the folds.*)

Yes, a cup of tea'll just do me, nice and 'ot and strong. Been drawin' since three o'clock, 'ave it.

That's right. The stuff they gives you at parish parties is something awful. 'Ot water it is, and not even always 'ot. I shall be in 'ot water myself at the vicarage, I expect, all along of me going to the Mothers' Meeting.

When she come herself to ask me, seein' as she was young and pretty like, I says 'Yes' to the new Vicar's lady, wishin' to oblige her, not as I'd any call to go to Mothers' Meetings, having brought up eight as is all going strong; but I'm that good-natured when not put upon.

So off I sets this afternoon with my best 'at, and I was trying to remember where the place was when I see a lady in the doorway, and she says to me, 'Are you coming to the meeting? You'll find it very interesting.' 'Well, I 'ad thought of it', I says, a bit doubtful; she was too civil for my taste.

'Please do', she says, 'we want such as you.'

'Lor', says I, took back. 'There's not much about it as I don't know.'

'Then you're one of us', says she, ''ow nice.'

She didn't look old enough to be married, let alone a mother, being a thin slip of a girl, and I thought she was kidding me, so I hesitated.

'We want more active members', she says, 'and there's so much food for discussion.'

I was glad to hear that, for they generally gives you only tea and buns, and I hadn't had much dinner.

'I don't mind 'elping to discuss it', says I, easy and pleasant like, 'and I'm active for my years though plumpish.'

The pore girl looked that pleased. 'Right', she says, 'you go in', and in I went.

It was a big 'all, 'alf full of women and some men, but no one seemed to be doin' no work, and a lady was on a platform talkin'. I sat down and listened, and, my goodness me, it was the rummiest Mothers' Meeting I ever see. The lady waved her arms up and down, and the things she said made me quite 'ot – to think as anyone could be so silly. Nicely dressed she were, too, in a big 'at with feathers and a lot of white fur.

''Ow', she says, 'do let us guard the sacred 'earths of 'ome.' No, 'oo wouldn't with a lot of babies about? 'Don't let us lose the respect of men by trying to enter the arena with them', as if we all wanted to be circus riders.

'The woman's fear[2] is the 'ome', she says, which sounded a bit dotty; 'let her stay in it and cherish it. The man goes out to fight – he is ready to give his life for his country, to bear 'ardships and suffering in the open field, while the woman who is otherwise constricted remains in the peaceful shelter of her 'ome. To 'im alone need be given the privilege of 'is constitooshun; while she should be content to be his 'elpmeet, not 'is compositor.'

'Let us 'ave fair play', says she, waving her arm emphatic, and then she went on about a lot of women as 'ad been in prison because they wouldn't pay their taxes, which didn't sound respectable, but she 'ad no call to go for 'em as she did.

'They abuse the very name of woman', she says, abusin' 'em
'erself all the time. 'They break the laws and is no credit to
their sects', though she didn't say whether they was chapel or
what. 'It's terrible', she says, in a low voice and staring at us
very persistent, 'to think 'ow these pore misguided crechurs
neglect their duties, and come forth into the public gaze, and
rant and rave on public platforms about their so-called rights.
Why do they interfere with pollytickle matters which pass their
understanding? It is not the woman's place – let her not enter
here.'

And she fixed me with her eye as she said it till I nearly called
out why did she do all these things herself if she didn't like it,
and I only come to please the Vicar's wife. Then she got on to
the law business, 'ow men made laws so well and careful for
women and knew so much better what we wanted than we did
ourselves, until my blood begun to boil, for to hear her talk
you'd think all men was angels and women just pet cats for 'em
to stroke when they'd a mind to. 'Fact is', she says very slow and
solemn, as if she'd just thought of something nobody'd ever
found out before, 'the 'ole jest of the matter lies in this, that
MAN IS MAN AND WOMAN IS WOMAN.'

Then she sits down sudden like, and I reely pitied her for giving
herself away before all of them mothers as needs no telling on
that point. There was a little clapping and someone else got
up and asked, 'As anyone something to say?' and no one said
nothing.

Me being of an inflannelettery nature, I got up but sat down
again, and some ladies in green dresses near me said, 'Go on,
speak up. Are you one of us?'

'I ain't one of her lot', says I. 'Then get up', they says, 'you wear
our colours, so speak out for us.'

I didn't know what they meant, but up I got, and however I
come to it I can't think; but I says, 'You may mean well, but
there's no sense in all you've been saying. What about the man
as can't or won't earn 'is living to keep 'imself and 'is family?
'Ow's the wife to stay quiet in 'er 'appy little 'ome as you

talked about if she's got a conic rhumyattic for 'er 'usband, as mine is, and has been for nine year? Where'd we be if I 'adn't buckled to and gone out to work for 'im and me and my eight kiddies?'

''Ear, 'ear', cries the ladies next me.

'Course', says I. 'I couldn't make as much as 'e did, along of me being only a woman, though I worked every bit as 'ard; they all said in the factory I was the better man of the two; and my Nellie as is a school teacher don't get near as much as Ernie who's a teacher too, though she's twice 'is brains. Seems to me that ain't fair play as you sets such store by.

'You talk of the man bearing 'ardship and suffering; what of the woman as bears children – no 'ardship and suffering about that, ain't there? Only she does it joyful for love of the little 'uns, and not for no privileges of constitooshun, which she ought to 'ave whatever they may be as much as anybody, seeing she risks 'er life every time she 'as a baby, and there's no Victorious Crosses nor no medals for 'er. Content to be 'is elp-meet – yes – but what when there's no meat to 'elp? Let's 'ave fair play by all means', says I. 'If you knew as much about men as I do you wouldn't be afraid of losing their respect. Ain't they glad to enjoy what we earn by going out? Let 'em fight when they've got to, though Government don't pay 'em too precious well for it', I says, 'as ought to know, 'aving two brothers and a nephew in the army. But I never come across a Tommy nor any other man as would refuse to eat a good dinner 'is mother or 'is wife 'ad earned by going out to work.

'And as for them pore things as has been in prison along of not paying their taxes, why should they pay 'em after all if they're not to 'ave nothing for it same as the men do? Not as I'm saying nothing against men nor 'aven't no call to', says I, 'orty like, 'seeing I've had two 'usbands and three sons as I'm proud of; but when it's taxes I don't see no difference between men and women. You can't even 'em up in one place and 'ave 'em top dog and bottom dog in another. That ain't fair play.

'Why', says I, 'you've 'eard a lot of talk, maybe, about Votes for Women. Not as I knows much about it; but I declare all you've been saying 'as just made me see clear that that's what we want.

Them laws, now. Why, do you know I ain't the parent of my own child by law! I 'ad such an argification over that with my first as would 'ave the boys brought up chapel, and I wanted 'em brought up church. He went off sudden with a popplelectic fit when they was babies, else there'd 'ave been ructions later. Then there's –' 'Sit down, please', says a lady on the platform, very indignant; but those near me was all smiling and clapping.

'I ain't near done', I says, feeling quite bold and cheerful, 'and it isn't manners to interrupt'; but lor, there was a regular 'ubbub, and they wouldn't let me go on.

The ladies near me come out with me and says: 'You are capital. Will you come to our meeting on Friday and speak for us?'

'No more Mothers' Meetings for me', says I, for I was put out in more ways than one.

'Ours is a Suffrage meeting', they says, 'not an Anti, like this.'

'A WHAT?' I says. 'This is Mrs Jocelyn's Mothers' Meeting, ain't it, as I've been to?'

Then they laughed ever so. 'Ours is an Anti-Suffrage meeting', they says, 'and that was Lady Clementina Pettigrew as was speaking when you came in. You 'ave took the wind out of her sails nicely.'

Well I never! To think of it! No matter, it was better than tea and buns.

The ladies took my name, and I've joined their society, as they said I must 'ave been one of 'em all along without knowing it, and I'm going to speak next Friday, and won't my old man be proud when he sees my name, Mrs Peter Puckle, on the posters.

And I 'ope you'll come and hear me. And I've got my colours.
See!

She pulls open her coat and displays the regalia of the WSPU.

Notes

1 Purple, green and white were the colours of the Women's Social
  and Political Union (WSPU).
2 A comedic misspelling and misunderstanding of the term 'women's
  sphere'.

An Anti-Suffragist *or* The Other Side

H. M. Paull

7 Advertisement for the Actresses' Franchise League Grand Matinee Musicale in 1910. The event was postponed from 10 to 24 May because of the death of King Edward VII. Courtesy of Mary Evans Picture Library/Women's Library.

H. M. Paull 1854–1934

Harry Major Paull was born in Monmouth on 6 January 1854, the son of Rev W. M. Paull. From 1871 to 1903 he worked at H. M. Office of Works and was Hon Secretary of the Dramatists Club from 1854 to 1934. Paull published over twenty plays and books between 1880 and 1930 including *The Great Felicidad* (1887), *Tenderhooks* (1889), *The Gentleman Whip* (1894), *The New Clown* (1902), *Hal, the Highwayman* (1904), *The Fortunes of the Fan* (1908) and three plays for all female casts: *The Last Day of Term* (1922), *Back to the College* (1923) and *Chums* (1925). He was a contributor to the *Nineteenth Century* and to the *Fortnightly Review* and his publications include *Literary Ethics* (1928) and *Bluff* (1928).

An Anti-Suffragist or *The Other Side* was published by the AFL in 1910.

'Miss De Lacey, the Secretary of the Little Pendleton
Anti-Suffragist Society, will now address the meeting.'

The reciter rises and speaks as follows:

Miss De Lacey   I should just like to tell you about the way in
which we started our Anti-Suffragist Society at Little Pendleton,
where I live. It's in the country of course, but we're not quite
out of the world; we're only 16 miles from Barchester; and we're
not so benighted that we haven't heard about the Suffragettes
and their horrid unladylike doings; though I don't see the paper
very often because papa always takes it with him when he goes
up to Barchester by the 9.40 every morning; and then mamma
and I feel free for the day.

But Miss Prideaux, a very rich maiden lady who lives at
the Hall, feels very strongly about the Suffragettes, and she
persuaded Lady Bellamy to have a drawing room meeting to
form an Anti-Suffrage Society.

Lady Bellamy is the daughter of a Duke and very exclusive; so
we all jumped at the idea of going to her house.

We talked about it day and night for a week, and all put on our
best frocks; and you may be sure we were at the Castle in good
time.

Lady Bellamy took the chair, but she didn't say much in her
opening speech, except that she didn't know anything about
politics, and she didn't suppose any of us did, but that she
was always pleased to do anything to elevate the masses;
which sounded rather patronizing. Then she called upon Miss
Prideaux to address the meeting.

Miss Prideaux wouldn't stand up to speak because she thought
it unladylike to be so obtrusive. She said that it was a great pity
that servant girls were getting so independent nowadays, and
she attributed it to the Suffragettes; and somehow she brought

in the comet, though I forget what that had to do with it. In her opinion Radicalism and Socialism were ruining the country, and she would never employ even a gardener on her place who didn't promise to vote Conservative. (And her gardens *are* beautiful you know.) It was the business of the men to make the laws, and women were quite unfit to take any part in politics. Then someone at the back with very bad taste asked whether Queen Victoria wasn't a political personage? And two irreverent girls giggled. But Miss Prideaux soon put the interrupter in her place; she said the question proved her point, because if the Queen had known anything about politics she never would have had Gladstone for a Prime Minister. And mamma said that was a very sensible remark.

Then one of the members for our division spoke; Sir Reginald Bellamy, a sort of cousin to Lady Bellamy. He's been divorced twice, so of course he knows something about women, and if he hasn't a high opinion of them you can't say it's from want of experience. He said that women have too much power as it is; that our function was to be charming and please the men; and that if we debased ourselves by interfering in politics and opposing men we shouldn't be treated with that consideration and deference which every English gentleman showed every woman. Well, of course that would be horrid, but everybody says he treated his wives shockingly; though I acknowledge he's gallant enough to all other women; in fact a great deal too gallant from all I hear; but I don't want to talk scandal. He went on to say women were frivolous and vain and hysterical and extravagant, and wanting in moral courage and a sense of responsibility and a lot more, til he made me feel more like a worm than ever.

He really was rather rude, and he ended up by saying that the fact that we had come here to assert how unfit we were to take any part in the affairs of our country showed that we agreed with him. Of course it would have been unladylike to contradict him, so we sat silent.

Then our other Member of Parliament spoke; he's a big mill owner. He said we must stand together back to back, as we were face to face with revolution.

Women in the mills were agitating for the same pay as the
men doing the same work, and he pointed out that that was
ridiculous; for if the women stayed at home they'd get no wages
at all, so anything he gave them was sheer profit to them. It
really was a treat to get an argument put so simply and clearly.

He gave us statistics too to prove that women did not want
the vote: I forget the exact figures but I think he said 103 per
cent didn't want it. And if the majority don't why should the
minority have it? That seems logical.

O, I forgot. He ended by saying that an election was coming on
soon, and he wanted us all to canvas for him and speak at his
meetings.

And the Archdeacon got up: a dear man, and so learned, but a
little absent-minded.

He quoted St Paul and Lord Curzon; I remember there was
something about long hair being a glory to us: the poor man is
quite bald. Then he said how the man was the natural master
of the house, and how woman's function was to obey; and we
all looked round to see if his wife was there but she wasn't,
lucky for him, for there's no doubt the dear man is dreadfully
henpecked, and if he wants to smoke he has to go to the
conservatory. He said woman's place was her home, and she
ought always to be found in it, not gadding about to meetings
and so on. That made me uncomfortable, for that's just what we
were doing. He said that a good woman would find plenty to fill
up her time if she fulfilled her duties to her husband and family.
That was a rather unfortunate remark, as Lady Bellamy is only
home three months in the year for the hunting, all the rest
of the time she's at Cairo or Monte Carlo or somewhere. He
told us it was man's function to govern and keep us unspotted
from the world; and that we ought to fight against the spirit
of rebellion and foster that of content. I do try to be content,
though it seems a little hard sometimes that papa allows Jack,
my brother in the army, £600 a year and I only get £45 and an
Xmas box of £10 if I've been good. But then, as mamma says,
Jack's a man, so that explains it. He got into debt badly last year

and papa had to pay a lot of money, nearly £1000, to put him straight; and when papa found I'd exceeded my allowance by nearly seven pounds he was awfully angry, and asked me if [I] wanted to ruin him, and docked it off this year's allowance; so I haven't been able to get a new hat this Spring.

But that hasn't anything to do with the meeting.

There was only one other speech, by General Sir Thomas Charrington; he's rather old and has only one lung, but he told us women couldn't fight and so we oughtn't to vote. Then someone said 'Joan of Arc', and Miss Prideaux said she was a French hussy who wore man's clothes; so that settled that. The General quoted these beautiful lines –

'O woman in our hour of ease

Uncertain, coy, and hard to please,

When pain and anguish wring the brow

A ministering angel thou.'[1]

Then he had a fit of coughing and his poor wife had to attend to him.

None of the ladies would speak, so Lady Bellamy said that they must appoint a Secretary, and to my horror she proposed me, and mamma accepted for me; I couldn't speak, I was blushing so.

Then came the question of subscription, and Miss Prideaux suggested five guineas so as to keep it select, and offered to give £100 to the funds if six other ladies would do the same, which was very generous of her, but so far we haven't got anyone to promise. Then Lady Bellamy said she must go as she was motoring to her sister's to tea; so we broke up though 'twas only half-past three, and they didn't give us any tea; and mamma and I had to walk home because Jack had the motor to go to golf.

He came back in an awful temper, for he'd had a match with Miss Vickers who plays for the county, and got licked at five and four to play; he said women had no business on the links.

We haven't had another meeting yet, as Lady Bellamy is away, but I quite hope that when she comes back in the winter we shall be able to fix a date. In the meantime I'm sure some of you will become anti-suffragists now you've heard the arguments; there's lots more, of course, and I've written to the Head Society to send me some but they haven't yet. O, and please let me have your subscriptions as soon as possible as I'm one and ninepence out of pocket already for postage. Still, it's in a good cause, and it's one's duty to do something useful in the world even if it does mean a lot of strain on one's brain; isn't it?

Note

1   Quote from Sir Walter Scott 'Marmion', Canto VI (1808).

Tradition

George Middleton

8 George Middleton (1880–1967), Dramatist. Photograph by
Arnold Genthe, 1915. Courtesy of Library of Congress,
Prints and Photographs Division.

George Middleton 1880–1967

Born in New Jersey in 1880, George Middleton was an American playwright and founder of the Dramatists Guild. He had over 20 plays produced, including *Criminals* and *Back of the Ballot* (both 1915); *Adam and Eva* (1919); *Polly with a Past* (1923), as well as publishing volumes of one-act plays. He married actress and suffragist Fola La Follette, the daughter of a progressive senator for Wisconsin, in 1911, and they both became speakers for the Suffrage cause. His memoir *These Things are Mine* was published in 1947.

Tradition was first performed at the Berkeley Theatre, New York City, on 24 January 1913 with the following cast:

George Ollivant   Mr George. W. Wilson

Emily, his wife   Miss Alice Leigh

Mary, his daughter, an actress   Miss Fola La Follette

Produced under the personal direction of Mr Frank Reicher.

Tradition was first published as part of Middleton's *One Act Plays of Contemporary Life* by Henry Holt and Company in 1913.

Scene: *The sitting room at the* **Ollivants'** *in a small town up state. It is an evening late in the Spring.*

A simple room is disclosed bearing the traces of another generation. Old fashioned window-doors at the right, overlooking the garden, open on a porch; another door in back opening on the hallway. A large fireplace at the left, now concealed by an embroidered screen; the horsehair furniture, several terra-cotta statuettes, and wood-cut or two on the walls create the subtle atmosphere of the past. There is a lamp on the table, and another on a bracket by the door in back. Moonlight filters through the window-doors.

The **Ollivants** *are discovered together.* **Mary,** *a rather plain woman of about 25, with a suggestion of quick sensibilities, is standing, lost in thought, looking out into the garden. Her mother,* **Emily,** *nearing 50, quiet and subdued in manner, is seated at the table trimming a hat. Occasionally she looks at* **Mary,** *stops her work, glances at her husband, closes her eyes as though tired, and then resumes. The silence continues for some time, broken only by the rattle of the town paper which* **George Ollivant** *is reading. He is well on in middle life, with a strong determined face not entirely without elements of kindness and deep feeling. When he finishes, he folds the paper, puts it on the table, knocks the ashes carefully from his pipe into his hand and throws them behind the screen; takes off his spectacles and wipes them as he, too, looks over towards his daughter, still gazing absently into the garden. Finally, after a slight hesitation, he goes to her and puts his arm about her; she is startled but smiles sweetly.*

Ollivant *(affectionately)* Glad to be home again, Mary?

Mary *(evasively)* The garden is so pretty.

Ollivant Hasn't changed much, eh?

Mary It seems different; perhaps it's the night.

Emily *(quietly)* This dry spell is not good for flowers.

Ollivant It's only the cultivated flowers that need care; can't help thinking that when I see the wild ones so hardy in my fields on the hill. (*Turning to* **Emily** *and patting her.*) Is there any of that spray mixture left, Emily, dear?

Emily   I haven't looked lately.

Ollivant   I'll order some to-morrow. (*Taking up his pipe again and looking for the tobacco.*) Think it would be a good idea, daughter, if you'd spray those rosebushes every couple of weeks. The bugs are a pest this Spring. Where's my tobacco?

Emily   On the mantel.

Ollivant   Wish you would always leave it on the table; you know how I hate to have things changed.

Ollivant *goes to the mantel, filling his pipe, and while his back is turned,* **Mary** *makes a quick questioning gesture to her mother, who sighs helplessly.* **Mary** *ponders a moment.*

Mary   How's Ben been doing these two years, father?

Ollivant   Hasn't your brother written you?

Mary   Only once – when I left home; he disapproved, too.

Ollivant   Had an older brother's feeling of wanting to take care of you, Mary.

Mary   Yes; I know. How's he doing?

Ollivant   He's commencing to get on his feet. Takes time and money for anyone to get started these days.

Mary   But he's still in partnership with Bert Taylor, isn't he?

Ollivant   Yes. He'd have been somewheres if he'd worked in with me as I did with *my* father. Things should be handed down. Offered him the chance, tried to make him take it, as your mother knows; but that college chum – nice enough fellow, I've heard – turned his head another way. (*Lighting his pipe and puffing slowly.*) It's best to humour a young fellow's ideas if he sticks them out, but I'd like to have had us all here together now. The place is big enough even if he should want to marry. Your mother and I came here, you know, when your grandfather was still alive.

Mary   Then Ben isn't making any money?

Ollivant (*reluctantly*)   Not yet – to speak of.

Emily (*quietly*)   But he's promised to pay his father back, Mary.

Mary   I see. (*Thoughtfully.*) College and then more help to get started, because he's a man.

Ollivant (*complacently*)   He'll have to support a family some day; I've had to keep that in mind.

Mary   I'd like to have a real talk with him.

Ollivant   When did his letter say he'd be coming for a visit, Emily?

Emily   The fifteenth.

Mary   Not till then? That's too bad.

Ollivant   Eh?

Mary (*after exchanging a quick glance with her mother, and gaining courage*)   Father, I hope you didn't misunderstand my coming back?

Ollivant   Not at all. We all make mistakes – especially when we're young. Perhaps I was a bit hasty when you left home, but I knew you'd soon see I was right. I didn't think it would take you two years – but perhaps if I'd written you before you'd have come sooner. I told your mother I'd like to make it easy for you to come home.

Mary   Mother suggested that you write me?

Ollivant   Well, I suppose you might put it that way. I always felt she thought I was a bit hard on you, but I'm not one to back down easily.

Mary   Don't blame me then, father, if I showed I was your daughter.

Ollivant   Let's forget my feeling; but naturally I was set back.

Mary   Because you didn't take my going seriously until I was actually leaving.

Ollivant   I couldn't get it into my head then, and I can't now, how any girl would want to leave a home like this, where you have everything. You don't know how lucky you are – or maybe you have realized it. Look about you and see what other girls have. Is it like this? Trees, flowers, and a lake view that's the best in the county. Why, one can breathe here and even taste the air. Every time I come back from a business trip it makes a new man of me. Ask your mother. Eh, Emily? When I sit out there on the porch in the cool evenings it makes me feel at ease with the world to know that the place is *mine* and that I've raised a family and can take care of them all. Ben had to go, I suppose – it's the way with sons; but I thought you, at least, would stay here, daughter, in this old house where you were born, where I was born, where all your early associations –

Mary (*shuddering*)   I hate associations.

Ollivant (*eyeing her*)   Well, I'd like to know where you get *that* from. Not from your mother and me. *We* like them, don't we Emily? Why, your mother's hardly ever left here – but you had to up and get out.

Mary   Yes. That's right, father; I *had* to.

Ollivant (*he stops smoking and looks at her sharply*)   Had to? Who made you?

Mary (*reluctantly*)   It was something inside me.

Ollivant (*in spite of himself*)   Tush – that foolishness.

Mary (*quickly*)   Don't make it hard for us again.

Ollivant   I made it hard, Mary? Because I objected to your leaving your mother here alone?

Mary   I remember; you said I was a foolish, 'stage-struck' girl.

Ollivant   Well, you're over *that*, aren't you?

Mary   That's just where you are mistaken, father. (*Slowly*) That's why I asked if you hadn't misunderstood my coming back.

Ollivant (*suspiciously*)   Then why did you come at all?

Mary   I'm human; I wanted to see you and mother, so I came when you generously wrote me. I'm not going to stay and spray the roses.

Ollivant (*he eyes her tensely and controls himself with an effort*)   So you are not going to stay with your mother and me?

Mary (*affectionately*)   I'll come see you as often as I can and –

Ollivant   – and make a hotel of your home? (**Mary** *is silent*) Don't you see your mother is getting older and needs somebody to be here?

Emily (*with a quiet assurance*)   I have never been so well and contented.

Ollivant (*tenderly*)   I know better, Emily; can't I see you're getting thinner and older? (*stopping her protests*) Now, let me manage this, dear. It's a girl's place to stay at home. You know my feelings about that. Suppose anything should happen to your mother, what would *I* do?

Mary   So it's not mother alone you are thinking of?

Ollivant (*tersely*)   I'm thinking of your place at home – doing a woman's work. I'm not proud of my daughter off earning her own living as though I couldn't support her.

Emily   George!

Mary   I thought it was only because I was on the stage.

Ollivant   Well, it's not the most heavenly place, is it? A lot of narrow-minded fools here in town thought I was crazy to *let* you go; I knew how they felt; I grinned and bore it. You were my daughter and I loved you, and I didn't want them to think any less of you by their finding out you were leaving against my wish.

Mary (*slowly, with comprehension*)   That's what hurt you.

Ollivant   Well, I blamed myself a bit for taking you to plays and liking them myself.

Mary   People here will soon forget about me and merely be sorry for you.

Ollivant (*persuasively*)   Why, Mary. I've made it easy for you to stay. I told everyone you were coming home for good. They'd think me a fool if –

Mary (*tenderly*)   You meant what was dear and good, father; but you had no right to say that. I'm sorry.

Ollivant   I did it because I thought you had come to your senses.

Mary (*firmly*)   I never saw so clearly as I do now.

Ollivant (*bluntly*)   Then you're stubborn – plain stubborn – not to admit failure.

Mary (*startled*)   Failure?

Ollivant   I know what the newspapers said; Ben sent them to me.

Mary   Which ones?

Ollivant   Why, all of them, I guess.

Mary   Did he send you the good ones?

Ollivant   Were there any?

Mary   Oh, I see. So Ben carefully picked out only those which would please you.

Ollivant (*sarcastically*)   Please me?

Mary   Yes: because you and he didn't want me to succeed, because you thought failure would bring me home. But don't you think I'll let some cub reporter settle things for me. I'll never come home through failure – never.

Ollivant (*kindly*)   Ben and I only want to protect you, Mary.

Mary   Why do men always want to protect women?

Ollivant   Because we know the world.

Mary   Yes: but you don't know *me*. Father, you still think I'm only a foolish stage-struck girl and want flowers and men and my name in big letters. It isn't that.

Ollivant   Well, what is it, then?

Mary   Oh – I want to be an artist. I don't suppose you can understand it: I didn't myself at first. I was born with it, but didn't know what it was till that first time you took me to the theater.

Ollivant   So it was all my fault?

Mary   It isn't anybody's fault: it's just a fact. I knew from that day what I wanted to do. I wanted to act – to create. I don't care whether I play a leading lady or a scrub-woman, if I can do it with truth and beauty.

Ollivant   Well, you haven't done much of either, have you? What have you got to show for our unhappiness? What have you got ahead of you?

Mary   Nothing – definite.

Ollivant (*incredulously*)   Yet, you're going to keep at it?

Mary   Yes.

Ollivant   What do you think of that, Emily?

Mary   I am going to the city Monday.

Ollivant (*persistently*)   But what will you do when you get there?

Mary   What I've done before: hunt a job, tramp the streets, call at offices, be snubbed and insulted by office boys – keep at it till I get something to do.

Ollivant   Come, come, Mary; don't make me lose patience. Put your pride in your pocket. You've had your fling. You've tried and failed. Give it all up and stay home here where you can be comfortable.

Mary (*with intense feeling*)   Father, I can't give it up. It doesn't make any difference how they treat me, how many times I get my 'notice' and don't even make good according to their standards. I can't give it up; I simply can't. It keeps gnawing inside me and driving me on. It's there – always there, and I know if I keep at work I will succeed. I know it: I know it.

Mary *throws herself into the chair, much stirred.* **Emily's** *eyes have eagerly followed her throughout this as though responding sympathetically, but* **Ollivant** *has stood in silence watching her apparently without comprehension.*

Ollivant (*not without kindness*)   Something inside. Huh! Have you any clear idea what she's talking about, Emily?

Mary *gives a short, hurt cry and goes quickly to the window, looking out and controlling herself with an effort.*

Emily (*softly as she looks at* **Mary**)   I think I understand.

Ollivant   I don't. Something inside. I never had anything like that bothering me. What's it all mean?

Emily (*quietly*)   So many people use the same words, but cannot understand each other.

Ollivant   Well, you seem to think it's mighty important, Mary, whatever it is; but it's too much for me. If you had something to show for it I wouldn't mind. But you're just where you started and you might as well give up.

Emily   George!

Ollivant   Now I don't know much about the stage, Emily, but Ben does. He says you're not made for an actress, Mary; you haven't got a chance.

Mary (*turning*)   Father!

Ollivant   Can't you see your failure isn't your own fault? If you were a beauty like Helen Safford or some of those other 'stars' – but you're not pretty, why, you're not even good-looking and –

Mary (*with bitter vehemence*)   Oh, don't go any further: I know all that. But I don't care how I look off stage if only I can grow beautiful on it. I'll create with so much inner power and beauty that people will forget how I look and only see what I think and feel. I can do it: I have done it: I've made audiences feel and even got my 'notice' because the stage-manager said I was 'too natural.' Helen Safford – what's she? A professional beauty with everything outside and nothing in. You think of her eyes, her mouth and her profile; but does she touch you so you remember? I know her work. Wait till I get a chance to play a scene with her – which they may give me because I'm not good-looking – I'll make them forget she's on the stage the first ten minutes – yes, and you and Ben, too, if you'll come. Helen Safford? Huh! Why, people will remember me when she's only a lithograph.

Ollivant   Well, then, why haven't you had your chance?

Mary (*quickly*)   Because most managers feel the way you and Ben do. And not having a lovely profile and a fashion-plate figure stands between me and a chance even to read a part, let alone play it. That's what eats the heart out of me, mother; and makes me hate my face every time I sit down to put on the grease paint.

Ollivant   Well, don't blame me for that.

Mary (*going to her mother, who takes her hand*)   You can laugh at me, father: You don't understand. It's foolish to talk. But, oh, mother, why is such beauty given to women like Helen Safford who have no inner need of it and here am I, with a real creative gift, wrapped up in a nondescript package which stands between me and everything I want to do? (*With determination*) But I will – ultimately I will make good, in spite of my looks: others have. And what I've suffered will make me a greater artist.

Ollivant (*in a matter-of-fact tone*)   Are you sure all this isn't overconfidence and vanity?

Mary   I don't care what you call it. It's what keeps me working.

Ollivant (*quickly*)   Working? But how can you work without an engagement?

Mary   That *is* the hard part of our life; waiting, waiting for a chance to work. But don't think I stand still when I haven't an engagement. I don't dare. That's why I keep at my voice work and dancing and –

Ollivant (*suddenly interrupting*)   Dancing and voice work when you have no engagements. Would you mind telling me who is paying the bills?

Mary (*indignantly*)   Father!

Ollivant   I think I have the right to ask that.

Mary   Have you?

Ollivant   I am your father.

Mary (*with quiet dignity*)   You thought you'd force me here at home to do as you wished because you paid for my food and clothes; when you took that from me you *ceased* to have that right. Don't forget since I left you've not helped me with my work or given me a penny.

Ollivant (*suspiciously*)   Mary . . . No, that's not why you went away from home?

Mary   No.

Ollivant   Or you met some man *there* and . . .

Mary   No.

Ollivant   There is some man.

Mary   Why a *man*?

Ollivant   Damn them; I know them. (*Breaking*) Good God, Mary, dear, you haven't . . . ? Answer me, daughter.

Mary (*calmly*)   No, there's been no need of that.

He has been violently shaken at the thought, looks at her intently, believes her, and then continues in a subdued manner.

Ollivant   Then who helped you? Ben?

Mary   How could he help me? Are men the only ones who help women?

Emily (*quietly*)   Tell him, Mary, it's best now.

Ollivant (*turning slowly to her in surprise*)   You know and have kept it from me?

Emily (*calmly as she puts down the hat she has been trimming*)   I found I hadn't lost my old skill, though it's been a good many years since I held a brush – since before we were married, George. I had an idea I thought would sell: paper dolls with little hand-painted dresses on separate sheets; they were so much softer than the printed kind and children like anything soft. I wrote to Mr Aylwin – you remember – he was so kind to me years before. He had called here once before when you were away and asked after my work. He used to think I had such promise. He found an opportunity to use the dolls as a specialty, and when I explained he induced some other firms to use all I can paint, too. They pay me very well. I made enough each month to help Mary when she went behind.

Ollivant (*incredulously*)   You! After you heard me say when she left I wouldn't give her a cent?

Emily (*looking fondly at* **Mary**)   You were keeping Ben, weren't you?

Ollivant   But – that's – that's different.

Emily   I didn't see why we shouldn't help *both* our children.

Ollivant (*perplexed by this as he turns to* **Mary**)   And you took it?

Mary   Yes.

Ollivant   You knew how she got the money?

Mary   Yes.

Ollivant   Your mother working herself sick for you, and you took it?

Emily   I told you I've never been so happy.

Mary (*simply*)   I couldn't bargain with what I felt. I had to study. I'd have taken anything, gotten it anywhere. I had to live. You didn't help me. Ben and I both went against your will, but you helped him because he was your son. I was only your daughter.

Ollivant *eyes her and seems to be struggling with himself. He is silent a long while as they both watch him. Finally, after several efforts he speaks with emotion.*

Ollivant   Mary, I – I didn't realize how much you meant to me till – till I thought of what might have happened to you without my help. Would – would you have stayed on in the city if – if your mother hadn't helped you?

Mary (*firmly*)   Yes, father: I would have stayed on.

Ollivant (*after a pause*)   Then I guess what you *feel* is stronger than all your mother and I tried to teach you . . . Are you too proud to take help from me – now?

Mary (*simply*)   No, father; till I succeed. Then I'll pay you back like Ben promised.

Ollivant (*hurt*)   You don't think it was the money, daughter? It would have cost to keep you here. It wasn't that.

Mary   No; it was your father speaking and his father and his father. (*Looking away wistfully.*) And perhaps I was speaking for those before me who were silent or couldn't be heard.

Ollivant (*with sincerity*)   I don't exactly understand *that* any more than the feeling you spoke of driving you from home. But I do see what you mean about brothers and sisters. You seem to think boys and girls are the same. But they're not. Men and women are different. You may not know it, but your mother had foolish ideas like you have when I first knew her. She was poor and didn't have a mother to support her, and she had to work for a living. She'd about given up when I met her – trying to work at night to feed herself in the day while studying. But she was sensible; when a good man came along who could support her she married him and settled down.

Look how happy she's been here with a home of her own that is a home with associations and children. Where would she be struggling to-day trying to paint pictures for a living? Why, there's lots of men who can paint pictures, and too few good wives for hard-working, decent men who want a family – which is God's law. You'll find that out one of these days and you'll give yourself as she did. Some day a man will come and you'll want to marry him. How could you if you keep on with your work, going about the country?

Mary (*quietly*)   You leave mother at times, don't you?

Ollivant   I've got to.

Mary   So may I.

Ollivant   And the children?

Mary   They'd have a share of my life.

Ollivant   A mighty big share if you're human, I tell you. Ask your mother if you think they're easy coming and bringing up.

Mary   And now they've left her. Dear mother, what has she to do?

Ollivant   Well, if you ever get a husband with those ideas of yours you'll see what a wife has to do. (*He goes to her.*) Mary, it isn't easy, all this you've been saying. But your mother and I are left alone, and perhaps we *have* got different views than you. But if ever you do see it our way, and give up or fail – well, come back to us, understand?

Mary (*going to him and kissing him*)   I understand how hard it was for you to say that. And remember I may come back a success.

Ollivant   Yes. I suppose they all think that; it's what keeps them going. But some day, when you're in love and marry, you'll see it all differently.

Mary   Father, what if the man does not come – or the children?

Ollivant   Why – (*He halts as though unable to answer her*)
Nonsense. He'll come, never fear; they always do.

Mary   I wonder.

Ollivant (*he goes affectionately to* **Emily**, *who has been staring before her during this*)   Emily, dear. No wonder the flowers have been neglected. Well, you'll have time to spray those roses yourself. I'll get the spray mixture to-morrow. (*Kisses her tenderly*) Painting paper dolls with a change of clothes! When I might have been sending her the money without ever feeling it. No more of that, dear; you don't have to now. I shan't let you get tired and sick. That's one thing I draw the line at. (*He pats her again, looks at his watch, and then goes slowly over to the window-doors*) Well, it's getting late. I'll lock up. (*Looking up at sky*) Paper says it will rain to-morrow.

Emily (*very quietly so only* **Mary** *can hear*)   At the art school they said I had a lovely sense of color. Your father is so kind; but he doesn't know how much I enjoyed painting again – even those paper dolls.

Mary (*comprehending in surprise*)   Mother! You, *too*?

Emily (*fearing lest* **Ollivant** *should hear*)   Sh!

Ollivant *closes the doors and eyes the women thoughtfully.*

Ollivant   Better fasten the other windows when you come. Good-night.

He goes out slowly as mother and daughter sit there together.

The curtain falls.

Further Reading

Arthur, Max. *Lost Voices of the Edwardians*. London: Harper Press, 2006

Auster, Albert. *Actresses and Suffragists: Women in the American Theatre 1890–1920*. New York: Praeger, 1984

Cockin, Katharine. *Women and Theatre in the Age of Suffrage*. Basingstoke: Palgrave, 2001

Cockroft, Irene and Croft, Susan. *Art, Theatre and Women's Suffrage*. London: Aurora Metro, 2010

Crawford, Elizabeth. *The Women's Suffrage Movement: A Reference Guide 1866–1928*. London: Routledge, 2001

Croft, Susan (ed.). *Votes for Women and Other Plays*. Twickenham: Aurora Metro, 2009

Engle, Sherry. *New Women Dramatists in America, 1890–1920*. New York: Palgrave Macmillan, 2007

Ferguson, Nigel. *Lost Empires: The Phenomenon of Theatres Past, Present and Future*. London: Cassell Illustrated, 2005

Friedl, Bettina. *On to Victory: Propaganda Plays of the Woman Suffrage Movement*. Boston: Northeastern University Press, 1987

Gale, Maggie. *West End Women: Women and the London Stage 1918–1962*. London: Routledge, 1996

Gale, Maggie and Gardner, Viv. *Auto/Biography and Identity: Women, Theatre and Performance*. Manchester: Manchester University Press, 2004

—. *Women, Theatre and Performance: New Histories, New Historiographies*. Manchester: Manchester University Press, 2000

Gillett, Paula. *Musical Women in England, 1870–1914: 'Encroaching on All Man's Privileges'*. New York: St. Martin's Press, 2000

Glenn, Susan A. *Female Spectacle: The Theatrical Roots of Modern Feminism*. Cambridge, MA: Harvard University Press, 2000

Hamilton, Cicely. *Marriage as a Trade*. London: Women's Press, 1981

Hayman, C. and Spender, D. *How the Vote Was Won: And Other Suffragette Plays*. London: Methuen, 1985

Holledge, Julie. *Innocent Flowers: Women in the Edwardian Theatre*. London: Virago Press, 1981

Kaplan, J. H. and Stowell, S. *Theatre and Fashion: Oscar Wilde to the Suffragettes*. Cambridge: Cambridge University Press, 1994

Liddington, Jill. *Rebel Girls: Their Fight for the Vote*. London: Virago, 2006
Liddington, Jill and Norris, Jill. *One Hand Tied Behind Us*. London: Virago, 1978
Lytton, Constance. *Prison and Prisoners*. London: Heinemann, 1914
McCarthy, Lillah. *Myself and My Friends*. London: Thornton Butterworth, 1933
Mackenzie, Midge. *Shoulder to Shoulder*. New York: Knopf, 1975
Middleton, George. *These Things Are Mine: The Autobiography of a Journeyman Playwright*. New York: Macmillan, 1947
Mitchell, Hannah. *The Hard Way Up: The Autobiography of Hannah Mitchell Suffragette and Rebel*. London: Faber and Faber, 1968
Moffat, Graham. *Join Me in Remembering: The Life and Reminiscences of the Author of 'Bunty Pulls the Strings'*. Cape Province, South Africa: W. L. Moffat, 1955
Moore, Eva. *Exits and Entrances*. London: Chapman and Hall, 1923
Nelson, Carolyn Christenson. *Literature of the Women's Suffrage Campaign in England*. Peterborough: Broadview Press, 2004
Stowell, Sheila. *A Stage of Their Own: Feminist Playwrights of the Suffrage Era*. Ann Arbor: University of Michigan Press, 1992
Tickner, Lisa. *The Spectacle of Women*. London: Chatto and Windus, 1987
Vanbrugh, Irene. *To Tell My Story*. London: Hutchinson and Co., 1948
Whitelaw, Lis. *The Life and Rebellious Times of Cicely Hamilton*. London: Women's Press, 1990

Sources for further information

The British Library, London
Ellen Terry Archive at Smallhythe Place, Kent
The Feminist Library, London
Library of Congress, Washington DC
Mander and Mitchenson Collection, Bristol University
New York Public Library
The Orlando Project – online database
Theatre Collection, V&A, London
The Women's Library, London
www.thesuffragettes.org